Central Park

Just Getting Started

Flowers

Just Getting Started

Tony Bennett

with Scott Simon

HARPER

An Imprint of HarperCollins*Publishers*

HarperCollins books may be purchased for educational, business, or sales promotional use. For information, please e-mail the Special Markets Department at SPsales@harpercollins.com.

FIRST EDITION

Designed by Leah Carlson-Stanisic

All artwork © Tony Bennett/Anthony Benedetto and used courtesy of Benedetto Arts, LLC. Likeness of Charlie Chaplin in rear endpaper, top right, courtesy of Charlie Chaplin™ © Bubbles Incorporated SA. All rights reserved.

Library of Congress Cataloging-in-Publication Data has been applied for.

ISBN 978-0-06-247677-7

ISBN 978-0-06-265394-9 (B&N signed edition)

ISBN 978-0-06-265819-7 (B&N Black Friday signed edition)

16 17 18 19 20   RRD   10 9 8 7 6 5 4 3 2 1

To my wonderful partner, Susan Benedetto

The Hills of Tuscany

Contents

Contents

Contents

The Plaza Hotel

Foreword

Tony Bennett has seen us through seven decades of life: falling in and out of love, breaking hearts, and many long, restless nights. That's what great singers do. They carry a tune for all of us. And no singer has carried more of our dreams for longer than Tony Bennett.

Tony Bennett has been my friend since the days of our youth and the streets of Queens. He was Anthony Dominick Benedetto when we were teenagers. Tony had to quit school and go to work as a singing waiter. That is your fate when your father dies young and your family needs money more urgently than you need a classroom. Soon, Tony was old enough to carry a rifle in a war that engulfed the world. He lived through desperate fighting at the battle's end, and was in a unit that liberated prisoners of a concentration camp. That taught Tony a lifelong lesson about the crime of hate.

When Tony got back from the war, he began to appear where he could do more singing than serving platters of pasta Bolognese. Pearl Bailey heard him once and asked him to join her at the Village Inn, downtown in New York. Who should come backstage one night but a guy Tony had once seen entertain thousands of other soldiers in Germany: Bob Hope.

He comes backstage and announces that he is not offering but telling Tony that he will sing in his shows at the Paramount Theatre. Means only a job as star. By the way, Hope says, he has a better name for the kid, who has been working under the stage name of Joe Bari, a show business name: "Tony Bennett. How do you like it?"

It turned out to be a name for now and forever. Ever since, on every day of his life, Tony Bennett has sung. And this great voice has not faded, from his first million-seller, "Because of You," a mere sixty-five years ago, until today, when he sings with a huge young talent with her own platinum records, Lady Gaga.

And there's no sign that he's running out. Tony Bennett today, an artist at age ninety, has a voice that soars as if he were twenty-five and still a kid, with young passion and love and a name that's still fresh on the scene. As Tony has gotten older, his voice has gotten finer, filled with more feeling with the more he's seen of life. That can't be said of any other singer. Tony Bennett's is a voice to reach from Astoria, Queens, to every corner of the city, the country, and the world. A voice in a book now, too, yes, to sing to us again, my friend.

—JIMMY BRESLIN

Just Getting Started

The Spanish Steps, Rome

Introduction

I know I'm lucky. I am lucky to have been born in America and in the most vibrant city in the world. I'm lucky to have had parents who loved me unreservedly, and though I lost my father when I was just ten, my mother devoted her life to me and my brother and sister. And I'm lucky to have had an older brother and sister who always looked out for me.

I'm lucky to have grown up during the Great Depression and now to live in a place that overlooks Central Park.

I'm lucky to have served in a war and survived. I know a lot of people who didn't.

I'm lucky to have lived to sing and make a living at it. I'm lucky to have come along at a time when I could sing some of the greatest songs of all time, by some of the greatest songwriters, and lucky to have worked alongside some of the truly great talents. I am lucky to have known, among so many names I cherish, Frank Sinatra, Duke Ellington, Ella Fitzgerald, Lady Gaga, Louis Armstrong, Amy Winehouse, and the queen of England (who is even a little older than me).

I am lucky to have found love and have four amazing children and seven incredible grandchildren.

I am lucky to have had success, lost my way, had some rough times, and been able to come roaring back. I am lucky to have met people all over the world and been able to bring something into their lives.

I am lucky to have worked with my pianist, Ralph Sharon, for fifty years, and that he found a song that he left for years in his shirt drawer called "I Left My Heart in San Francisco." And I'm lucky to still be working with magnificent musicians who tour with me along the way through so many great venues around the world.

I am lucky to still be singing, performing, and entertaining people all over the world at an age that is long after many great performers have retired. And I'm just getting started.

This book is about people who have helped, influenced, and steered me along the way. Some, like my parents, I knew very well. A few I didn't know at all. But I've been lucky that their lives, their work, their words, their example have helped inspire and steer me.

I've learned a lot about singing from composers and instrumentalists, but also from artists, painters, and looking at the trees in Central Park. And I've learned a lot about life from my own family, the people with whom I've worked, names you've heard and those you haven't, and people I've met along the road and on the street (and these days by e-mail). I hope I've learned from my own experiences and even—especially—from my own mistakes. As I come singing, happily and steadily, into my ninety-first year, this book is about some of the lives that have made mine the blessing it has been to me.

No one is alone—onstage or in life. A singer is lucky to be in the spotlight. But each breath and note are a partnership between the talents who write the song, the musicians who bring it alive, and only then—finally—the man or woman who gives the song a voice. I try to put everything into that song—and into life.

Life abounds with lessons, if we're lucky enough to be alert to them. But they're not always what we think they're about. Experiences leave marks in our minds and hearts. Years later, we find that they snap into place.

Tuscany

Anna Suraci Benedetto

My mother taught me the most important lesson of my life: quality lasts.

My mother, Anna Suraci Benedetto, sewed dresses. She worked in a factory by day and brought home dresses at night because she was paid by the piece and had to support my brother, my sister, and me. My father had died when I was ten. Every night, we'd meet my mother at the Ditmars Boulevard el train stop, the north terminal of the lines from Queens, when she returned from Manhattan and help her carry home a big bundle of unsewn dresses. We'd climb the stairs, and she'd start to sew as soon as she got home. She'd stop to make us dinner, and after that, while we kids read or listened to music, she would bend over her sewing machine again to continue stitching dresses.

Sometimes she'd get her thumb caught under the sewing needle. She'd cry out in pain but put on a bandage and go back to work. She couldn't afford to stop. Watching her made me vow, in my heart, to be so good at something I loved that my mother wouldn't have to work again.

I sat next to my mother as she worked, just to be near her, and every now and then she'd pick up a new dress to be sewn, feel the cloth between her fingers, and set it aside with a frown.

She'd say, "I only work on quality dresses."

Our family needed every dime my mother would get to stitch one more piece. But my mother would not sew a dress that was not up to her standards. She showed me that people should take pride in what they do.

Cipriani Garden, Venice

I thought of my mother years later as I began my career, enjoyed success, and encountered setbacks. I was determined to be so successful to make up for all my mother had sacrificed for us. I never wanted her to have to bend down over another sewing machine again, except to sew something for her grandkids. But when a producer or promoter would tell me that I needed to record a song I considered cheap, shoddy, silly, or senseless, I'd think of my mother and tell him, in so many words, "Sorry, I only work on quality material."

My mother, the seamstress, taught me a life lesson about art that I've learned applies to life and love, too: hold out for quality. You might have to work a little harder. It will take a little longer. But you will produce something that lasts.

New York City Snowstorm

2

Bob Hope

I owe Bob Hope my name and in some ways my life in show business. In the winter of 1945, I was barely twenty, a kid from Queens and in the front lines in Germany. I was in G Company of the 255th Regiment, 63rd Infantry Division, Seventh Army.

The Germans had 88-millimeter cannons that shot shells that whistled with a terrifying hiss before they hit, throwing fire and hot metal into the air. We had to dig foxholes for shelter, which could take hours, shovel by shovel, to chip and dig into the frozen ground. We couldn't light fires to keep warm—even the light of a single cigarette could tell the enemy where we were—so we just clawed ourselves close to the cold ground and shivered in the foxhole, in snow or bone-chilling rain, for twelve or sixteen hours, until it was light.

Sometimes we'd hear Germans whispering to each other. I'm sure they could hear us, too, but nobody wanted to get up and start shooting. We just wanted to make it through the night alive.

We'd wake up when those huge, loud shells went off and listen for screams. Sometimes we'd get up and find out who had died.

I hated war and have always wondered why they produce horror films with make-believe monsters but call war movies "adventure stories." There is nothing adventurous about combat. When you're in the front lines, you wake up every day and wonder if it will be your last. You march and wonder if each step you take is your last. You question why people who were next to you, whom you didn't know long enough to even know their names, have died while you're still alive. You wonder if you'll be next. It's hard to see all that dying and suffering and think you'll get out.

One day our officers told us to get out of the front line and into some trucks. We assumed we were going to be sent somewhere even tougher, to replace a lot of soldiers who had already died. Then an officer told us, "You boys are gonna see a show!"

That's when we saw Bob Hope.

Thousands—tens of thousands—of us must have been there, though Bob would have hopped down from a truck and done a show for a dozen GIs if they'd asked. All of us soldiers were grimy, frightened, and exhausted. Bob and other stars he'd brought along, including Jane Russell and Jerry Colonna, and of course Les Brown's band, were just small figures on a stage far away. But Bob and his friends made us laugh. I don't think I remember a single joke. But I'll never forget how wonderful it felt to laugh through the whole show. The dread, fear, and worry just rolled off of us in waves of laughter.

A lot of us knew Bob from the movies, of course, but he was also the biggest radio star in America then. Just to hear the voice we remembered from our living rooms come to us in person in that hellish landscape in Germany reminded us of home and family, our parents and sisters, our neighborhoods and friends. Bob and his crew helped us remember why we were trying so hard to stay alive. On that afternoon with Bob Hope, I saw how much songs and a show can give to people.

The war ended before I could get hurt—I think that's how every GI felt. Relief, not triumph. I was alive, while other people—good, brave, and kind people, on both sides—had died. War forces you to take hold of the life you've been given and try to do something with it, enjoy it, and help others.

I stayed on as part of the troops who occupied Germany and began to sing for my supper while still in uniform. I was assigned to the 314th Army Special Services Band of the European theater, and we did a show every Sunday night from the Wiesbaden opera house called *It's All Yours.*

The show was meant to be a breath of home for the GIs serving in Germany and a small slice of America for German civilians, who were glad the war was over but not so happy to be occupied. But American music had been popular before the war, and we picked right up with it. Jazz and swing, more than ever, seemed wild, free, and the sound of the future.

We had some great musicians who were doing their time in uniform, including Dick Stott, the sax player, and George Masso, a trombonist who would become a great orchestrator. We played every kind of music, from light classical to swing and dance, and there were no restrictions—no playlists, no focus groups, no charts or surveys—to tell us what songs we could or couldn't play. If we liked a song, it went into the show, and that was a freedom I wound up fighting for all through my career.

Every now and then, Bob Hope would bring a USO tour through town and make a guest appearance on our show, but I never really met him.

It was after I got back to the States and started appearing

in clubs as Joe Bari—lots of the time for free—that our paths crossed. Joe Bari was a stage name I had given myself before the war. Performers at the time were told to avoid long names or names that screamed ethnicity. (Ethnic names have made their ways onto marquees by now. But short ones—Adele, Beyoncé, Eminem, Lady Gaga—still prevail.) I came up with "Bari"

West Side Blues

because if I wasn't going to have an identifiably Italian name, I could at least give it a flavor. So I pieced together the last letters of Calabria, where my grandparents had been born. And you don't get any more American than Joe.

One night in 1949, the great Pearl Bailey heard me sing and liked me, and she made me part of her show at the Village Inn downtown. That same month, in November, Bob Hope came to New York to play the Paramount. He had an old performer on his payroll named Charlie Cooley, who had once given him a break, and Bob had made him part of his entourage. Charlie came to see Pearl, and I was lucky enough to open her show. Charlie had a good time and liked what he saw. He brought Bob down to see us, too.

I was sitting in my dressing room between shows when the best-known profile in America walked in.

"C'mon, kid," Bob said. "You're going to come to the Paramount and sing with me." It was like telling a minor leaguer he was being called up into a game at Yankee Stadium.

"But I don't like your stage name," he told me. "What's your real name?"

Bob himself had been born Leslie Townes Hope in London. "What's your real name?" was a common topic of conversation in dressing rooms and on tour buses.

"My name is Anthony Dominick Benedetto," I told him.

"Too long for the marquee," Bob told me, and after a pause he announced, "We'll call you Tony Bennett."

And here I am—Tony Bennett for all time—at the age of ninety.

Bob Hope showed me real showmanship. He was a showman in every sense of the word. No one made more jokes than Bob himself about how many writers he had to make him sound clever and funny. But he was sharp and droll on his own, too.

He was a total entertainer. All of Bob's Oscar jokes aside—
"Or, as we call the Oscars in my house, Passover"—a song he
sang with Shirley Ross, "Thanks for the Memory" (by Ralph
Rainger and Leo Robin) won the 1938 Academy Award for
Best Original Song and became Bob's signature. He was first a
hit in vaudeville as a dancer, in an act that included the Hilton
Sisters, who were famous conjoined twins.

He was also a good athlete—a golfer as he got older but a
boxer in his youth—and nobody owned a stage like Bob Hope.
He showed me how to walk out onto the stage and let people
know you're happy and ready to entertain them. He taught me
how to look like there's no place you'd rather be. It's usually
true.

To be on Bob's show included singing with the fabulous Les
Brown and His Band of Renown. It was the first time I ever
sang with a major band, and I learned a lot from those talented
musicians. When I finished my first song, Bob sauntered out
onto the Paramount stage with his distinctive strut, waited for
the applause to fade, and told his fans, "Well I was getting tired
of Crosby anyhow."

He wasn't, of course. But he knew it was the kind of compliment for a newcomer that would get quoted and passed along.
It helped the audience root for me.

I joined Bob and the rest of his troupe for a six-city tour after
we finished the run at the Paramount. People use the term "like
a rock star" far too much these days, but I tell you that when
Bob Hope was on tour, there was usually more excitement than
there would be for most presidents or royalty. Bob flew his show
from city to city, at a time when most tours were still by train
(his work for the USO had showed him how much more ground
you could cover by airplane). The local police would stop traffic and whisk us to the theater in city after city. We wound up

on the West Coast and on Bob's radio show. I didn't get to sing on his show then. But I got to hang out at the studio, see some of the magic that made it so popular, and meet all kinds of talented people who had just been famous names to me until then.

I was in the studio one day when Bob introduced me to a man who was at the center of a circle of people. It was Bing Crosby. It was like a young ballplayer getting to shake hands with Joe DiMaggio.

Do you know what I think I learned most from Bob Hope? He never forgot a favor. Anyone who had given him a break or done him a favor, any of the singers, dancers, or smiling gals who had joined him on a USO tour, knew that Bob wouldn't just say good-bye and forget about them. He'd work them into one of his movies or television specials. He'd take them on tour. I saw Bob Hope from a long way off when I was a young GI. He reminded me of home and gave me a glimpse of what a gift song and laughter can be to others. Then I met him, and he gave me the name by which I'm known today and opened the door to the blessed life I've had in this business. I hope I've repaid his confidence and kindness.

Palmilla los Cabos, Mexico

3

Bing Crosby

I wish I could say that when I shook hands with Bing Crosby at Bob Hope's radio studio, he looked at me and said, "Tony, there's just one thing I want to tell you . . ." It would have been nice to have that memory. But Bing didn't have to tell me—or any singer—anything at all. He *showed* us all how it was done, from singing to choosing songs to picking collaborators. Music, films, recording—nothing was the same after Bing.

Every singer who uses a microphone owes something to Bing Crosby. A lot of singers saw microphones and figured all they had to do was stand back and sing as they always had, puff out their chests and let fly to reach the back of the house. Bing saw that the microphone could put your voice right next to someone's ear. It could make singing more intimate, even conversational.

So Bing brought the microphone close and relaxed his voice, which gave it more warmth. He sang as if he were speaking into the ear of a lover. He made the microphone into an instrument for intimacy.

They called his style crooning, but he never liked that term. It was a whole new style that stressed words, phrasing, melody, and *feeling.*

(It's hilarious to read today some of the warnings of public moralists of the 1930s about how crooners would lead our kids into vice and depravity. Bing Crosby? The guy in the golf sweater?)

Bing was big in a way that's hard to grasp these days. In 1931, when I was six and just beginning to listen to the radio in Queens, he had ten of the top thirty songs of the year, including "I Found a Million Dollar Baby (in a Five and Ten Cent Store)." By 1936, he was hosting the Kraft Music Hall (opening the show with "Where the Blue of the Night Meets the Gold of the Day"—people all over America could sing those lines like they do commercial jingles now) and was making three films a year, including *Pennies from Heaven*, which featured the song that became a Depression-era ballad.

Bing also made what would become a typically wise business decision. Singles cost a dollar in those days. A dollar is usually what it costs to download a single song in these modern, much more expensive times. But few people could afford to pay a dollar for music during the Depression. Record sales plummeted.

Jack Kapp, the founder of Decca Records, decided, in so many words, that if you can't sell your salami for a dollar, you lower the price until it moves. He decided to charge 35 cents for a single and pay performers and composers a royalty for each record sold, rather than a flat fee for recording.

A lot of artists balked; it might lower their incomes (or increase them, of course, depending on sales). But Bing saw that there would be no market for music if people couldn't afford to buy records. Radio was already bringing music into their homes for free. Bing stayed with Decca and supported Jack Kapp's idea, and, given that he was the number one–selling recording artist in America, he essentially rescued the record industry. And did pretty well for himself, too.

Every kid in America and his grandfather could hum "Buh-bu-bu-booo . . ." You knew they were imitating Bing. He was the number one talent on radio, on records, and in movies all at the same time, when everyone in America, more or less, listened to many of the same songs and saw many of the same movies.

The Beatles, Elvis Presley, Bob Dylan, and Madonna have all been huge. But no less than the ranking Beatle, Sir Paul McCartney, will tell you that Bing was the breakthrough. In a way, he made all of our careers possible.

Bob Hope has received a lot of praise for entertaining troops overseas, often near the front lines. And he should. But Bing (and Dorothy Lamour, Jerry Colonna, Les Brown, and a lot of others) were often with him, almost step for step. I wouldn't call Bing a political person. But he had convictions.

He began his career in his hometown of Spokane, Washington. Mildred Bailey, a great Seattle blues and jazz singer I came to admire, was a huge influence on Bing. He began to sing on the same bill as her brother Al Rinker. Bing returned the favor by introducing her to the bandleader Paul Whiteman, and Mildred began to tour with Paul's band. Mildred happened to be a registered member of the Coeur d'Alene tribe and worked at a music store in Seattle that sold records and sheet music. That's where, according to the story, Bing first heard the records of Louis Armstrong and other black jazz greats from Chicago, Harlem, and New Orleans.

Listen to Louis's recording of "Lazy River," especially when he leans into a low, rich growl to sing "Throw away your troubles / Dream a dream of me . . ." See if you don't hear a little of the beginnings of the "Buh-bu-bu-booo . . ." by which Bing would be so identified.

Bing admired Louis Armstrong as an artist and then got to know and adore him as a friend. Bing wanted Louis to have a featured role in *Pennies from Heaven*, but Harry Cohn, the head of Columbia Pictures (who people said kept a picture of Mussolini in his office, just to show he meant business), said

Monet Garden #5

no. Bing walked out. Harry Cohn gave up. Louis appeared in the film, and Bing made sure he got equal billing alongside the other (white) costars.

I was privileged to sing with some of the same great jazz musicians who played with Bing, and I don't recall that they ever had a story that went, "So Crosby took out his pipe and told me . . ." That's not how inspiration works. You hear the immense influence of Bing Crosby when you listen to Frank Sinatra, who came along a decade later, and Nat "King" Cole, who was just a little behind Frank, and then me, who was another decade behind them. We were all singers of popular songs who loved and respected jazz and tried to bring it into our music. Bing said he sang only songs that he liked, and, like a jazz artist, he tried to bring something different to a song each time.

Even into my nineties, I'll do more than one hundred shows in any given year. I'll be in the studio with Lady Gaga, John Mayer, k.d. lang, and Queen Latifah. I'll sing the songs I love and have sung a thousand times. But I'll try to do a little something different each time and on each take.

There is always something new to learn. There is always something new to try.

New York Rainy Night

4

Louis Armstrong

I never met a man who wore genius with as light a touch as Louis Armstrong. It's impossible to imagine him without that broad, almost blinding smile he was known for—the sheer, clear pleasure he took in playing and singing and being onstage.

Louis was the grandson of slaves, and had grown up in a neighborhood so tough it was known as "the Battlefield." Today the international airport of his hometown is Louis Armstrong International because his name (and nickname, Satchmo) is still celebrated around the world as an example of American genius.

Louis Armstrong invented jazz as much as the Wright brothers invented the airplane—in other words, although hundreds of other worthy people made important contributions to America's defining music, Louis was the one who made it soar.

I once painted a portrait of Louis Armstrong while we were both in London and gave it to him. He brought it back home and hung it in his study in Sunnyside, Queens, where he lived. Louis would tell visitors, "Here's a painting a guy who lives in my neighborhood did of me."

Louis had a life made for the blues, and turned it into jazz. When Louis was just a baby, his father left the family. For years thereafter, he'd only get a glimpse of the man he was told was his father when he played music in New Orleans parades. His mother, Mary, worked as a prostitute in Storyville, a red-light district of New Orleans where the trade was tolerated. To help support his mother and sister, young Louis worked a series of hard jobs, such as hauling coal to homes, before he was even a teenager. But the brothels of Storyville were overflowing with music, and Louis joined other boys in the neighborhood who sang for money.

How did the greatest trumpet player alive first play the horn?

William Gary "Bunk" Johnson, a great trumpet player, claimed to have first shown young Louis how to play by ear at a place called Dago Tony's. But Bunk, who had career resurgence in the 1940s, was famed for his storytelling. Louis always credited the great (and much more famous) Joe "King" Oliver, who was certainly his mentor. But then Louis, bless him, was famed for his storytelling, too. For years he told interviewers that he had been born on the Fourth of July; baptism records later revealed he was really born on August 4, 1901. To which I say, the day Louis Armstrong was born ought to be a national holiday in any case, so I'd go with July 4—and King Oliver—too.

There was also a Jewish family, the Karnofskys, with a junk-hauling business in the neighborhood, who gave Louis odd jobs to do for money and, more important, clothes and meals in their home. They became a kind of family for Louis, not replacing his mother, but becoming a part of his life, too. Louis wore a Jewish star all of his adult life, in tribute to the family he had been part of. He liked to remind people that Jews had not had an easy time of it in most of New Orleans, either.

Louis was spirited, creative, rambunctious, and ambitious.

Sometimes his rambunctiousness (he fired a pistol into the air on one of the city's many holidays) got him sent to the New Orleans Home for Colored Waifs. There, a wonderful musician, Professor Peter Davis, who came to the school several times a week, showed young Louis some of the technical skills, including reading music, which polished his creative genius. Louis became the bandleader of the home's orchestra, and featured cornet player, as they played in parades and other gigs.

By the time he was fourteen, Louis Armstrong was playing aboard riverboats and in bands with Bunk Johnson and his idol, King Oliver. King took off for Chicago when Louis was nineteen, and left him in charge of what was left of his band. Three years later, the King asked him to come north. Chicago had the most vibrant jazz scene in the country then, and Louis's days of taking odd jobs to make ends meet were over. In fact, he quickly became pretty rich.

"It was the first time I lived in my own apartment," he once told me, "with my own bathtub, my own bathroom."

By the time I met Louis Armstrong, he was in his late forties and had been the face of jazz for a generation. He had also become known as Satchmo and Pops, beloved nicknames that had been given to him for his wise, folky observations, like, "You blows who you is," and, "If you have to ask what jazz is, you'll never know," and, "If they act too hip, they play like shit."

(One version of how he got the nickname Satchmo comes from a story he told, that when he used to dance for pennies on the streets of New Orleans, he had to scoop up pennies from the street before older boys could steal them, and became known as Satchelmouth. At other times he said the name came from his wide, warm grin. But I'm not sure even Louis knew. Or if he did, that he'd tell us.)

He had also made scores for recordings and films, been on

the cover of *Time*, been a worldwide ambassador of jazz for the United States, and received a golden trumpet from King George V.

Louis Armstrong essentially created the role of soloist in jazz. His trumpet artistry and ingenuity were so distinctive, they couldn't be contained. Great classical players would hear Louis play and ask, "How does he do that?" But in creating that role for the horn, he also carved out a place for the individual voice of the singer in jazz. He took some of the most popular songs of the day, ran them through his genius, and turned them into something totally different. "Never do it the same way twice," Louis always said.

And of course . . . what a voice Louis Armstrong had! It was gravelly and raspy, but also revealing and expressive. Louis told me once he had begun singing a verse or two in a song to save wear and tear on his mouth and lips from blowing the horn; then people began to ask him to sing. His singing became inseparable from the rest of his artistry.

Think of George Douglas and George David Weiss's great song "What a Wonderful World." We've all recorded it. But in your mind, do you hear anyone but Louis Armstrong singing it? ABC Records didn't like it and didn't promote it when it came out in 1967. But then it zoomed to the top of the charts in Britain, got more play in the United States, and zipped to the top here, too. What you hear in Louis's singular rendition is the voice of a man who was born into hard times but made a joyful life. When he sings, "What a wonderful world!" you believe it.

Louis was a good friend of my pal Bobby Hackett, the great horn player who also lived in Queens. They'd spend hours listening to classical music together. When they came over to my house once, Louis said, "I'm the coffee, Bobby's the cream." His gift for expression was always on.

Louis's smiles were sincere. But he had also learned, a long time before, how the light he could shine on others with his talent and zest could shield him from some of the hurts of the outside world.

In the 1960s, some young black activists criticized Louis. They considered his ceaseless grin to be a kind of shucking and jiving for whites. But where were they in 1957, when Louis refused to go on a State Department tour to perform in the Soviet Union because he felt that President Eisenhower and the federal government were not coming to the aid of the nine black students who had been enrolled at Little Rock Central High School?

"The way they are treating my people in the South, the government can go to hell," Louis told reporters. "It's getting so bad, a colored man hasn't got any country." And by the end of the month, President Eisenhower sent in the 101st Airborne Division to protect the black students and their place in the school. When pundits said that public opinion had forced Ike to send in troops, I couldn't think of a more powerful opinion than Louis Armstrong's. His warmth and smiles were utterly sincere. But so was his rare, righteous anger.

I think what I learned most from Louis is how, by taking joy in your work, you can give joy to others. So many performers somehow behave as if their talent were some kind of a burden or a chore, from which they can never take a rest. Louis Armstrong's enthusiasm for using and sharpening the talent he had to entertain others was unquenchable and, for those of us blessed to know him, almost contagious. Louis' memory reminds us to make the most of what we are given while we can, and to spread it generously.

New York

5

Fiorello La Guardia

The first politician I really remember is Fiorello La Guardia, and what a memory that is to have. I wasn't even ten years old on the day we met him in 1936. He stood just five foot two, barely taller than I was at the time. To this day, he is the standard by which I instinctively measure all politicians.

La Guardia (nicknamed "the Little Flower," which is the meaning of *Fiorello* in English) was a Republican who loved FDR and the New Deal, a progressive who took on Tammany Hall and Democratic political corruption, an Italian American who took on Lucky Luciano and organized crime. La Guardia was the product of an ethnic stew in his own family, with an Italian Catholic father and Triestine Jewish mother, and he reached out with respect and jobs to uplift the new immigrants who were flooding into New York. You can still see his hand on the amazing, aging infrastructure of modern New York.

My uncle Frank Suraci, my mother's brother, was a staunch Republican who helped deliver votes for La Guardia in our neighborhood of Astoria, Queens, during the 1933 election for mayor. Uncle Frank had often arranged for my older brother, Johnny, to sing at local Republican functions (people called Johnny "Little Caruso").

When La Guardia was elected mayor, Uncle Frank was rewarded with the job of library commissioner for the borough of Queens. Politics or show business, it never hurts to do favors.

One of Fiorello La Guardia's promises as mayor was to complete the Triborough Bridge, which would connect Manhattan, Queens, and the Bronx. Construction had begun in 1929, but was suspended after the stock market crash and the United States sinking into the Great Depression. Because La Guardia had cemented a working relationship with President Franklin Delano Roosevelt, who had come into the White House shortly before La Guardia was elected, he convinced him to commit millions of dollars from the New Deal's new Public Works Administration to finish the bridge. In a way, the bridge's completion declared that New York was back in business.

The ribbon to open the bridge was to be cut on July 11, 1936. President Roosevelt spoke from a podium. Uncle Frank, as usual, arranged the entertainment. Around that time, my brother, Johnny's, voice began to change with adolescence. He gave up singing just as I was getting seriously interested in music and songs. (Inspired by my brother's example, I had begun to sing, too, although Johnny sang opera, while I mostly sang pop tunes. A great teacher at my grade school, Mrs. McQuade, took an interest in me and my singing and drawing. She made me feel talented and special. Mrs. McQuade had arranged for me to sing a few times at the local Democratic club, which, as I look back on it, must have put Uncle Frank in an awkward position.)

But Uncle Frank gave me my first Republican gig, when he arranged for me to sing at the bridge opening ceremony, three weeks before my tenth birthday. I wore a little white silk suit stitched by my mother. I wound up standing next to Mayor La Guardia as he cut the ribbon and sang "Marching Along Together" ("Singing all along the line / What do we care for weather? / We'll be there in rain or shine") as the mayor and I and thousands of other people walked over the bridge.

The biggest man in town (even though he was just five foot two) and a little boy in a white suit opening a great bridge. What a day when you're not even ten years old—or ninety.

La Guardia was such a bright, bustling, dynamic presence. He loved people. You sensed that although he enjoyed the attention he received on the public stage, he was on that stage to help people. As much as Franklin D. Roosevelt, Fiorello La Guardia gave people hope in fearful times. All of us who are onstage for a living can hope that, now and again, we can do that, too.

The Triborough Bridge that Mayor La Guardia and I opened in 1936 was officially renamed the Robert F. Kennedy Bridge in 2008, although most New Yorkers still call it the Triborough. But I want to take advantage of my "special relationship" with that bridge to say I think the name change is fine and fitting. Robert F. Kennedy was one of the few politicians who ever measured up to Fiorello La Guardia.

Tuscany

6

Pyrites

I t was a small mill town fifteen miles from the Canadian border when I lived there for nine months as a boy. It's classified as a hamlet of the town of Canton, New York, now, and I went to live there under just about the worst of circumstances.

I was ten years old, and my father had just died. He loved art and music, Gandhi and Paul Robeson; he was strong and sensitive and the center of my world. Then he died of congestive heart failure. His brother, my uncle Dominick, came to my mother after the funeral and said it would be tough to be a thirty-six-year-old working single mother and widow with three kids. Why didn't she send me to live with him and his wife in their small town in upstate New York?

I thought it was a terrible idea. I was ten and had just lost my father. How could it possibly help to be without my mother, too? I think the idea of being apart also tore at my mother. But in some ways it also sounded so appealing, the fresh air, blue skies, and quiet roads of the country. She must have seen it as the best thing she could do for me, because that's what she always wanted.

So off I went, ten years old, with a suitcase, leaving my family in Queens behind. Uncle Dominick and Aunt Dominica owned the general store in Pyrites and had a farm. They'd never had children and didn't seem to know what to do with me. I gladly helped out with farm chores, but Uncle Dominick was upset to come home one day and find me singing in the kitchen to Aunt Dominica as she ironed. He must have had a hard day in the fields. He saw me singing to my aunt and just kicked the chair out from under me and screamed, "Why don't you do some work around here? Why don't you milk a cow or something?"

Singing gave me joy. It reminded me of my father, the man I so admired, and the stories I had heard about him singing before his sickness weakened his lungs. Getting my chair kicked out from under me by my uncle Dominick made me miserable all over again and made me wonder, what was I doing with them in this place called Pyrites?

I tried to spend most of my time with my cousins, the Futias, who lived next door, especially my favorite cousin, Mary Lou. I went to school with Mary Lou and her brothers and sisters. My singing was appreciated there. Parents would come up to me after school plays and ask me to sing some of the latest hits. They'd dig into their pockets to give me change. I was the kid from New York, and I guess they thought I was a little big-city entertainment. In some ways, Pyrites was my first out-of-town gig. Well, it was a tough one.

I was there an entire school year, and then my mother brought me back home—home to Astoria, Queens.

Nine months seems like a century to a ten-year-old. I see now that it must have seemed even longer to my mother, losing her husband and then missing a son. It's been a hard story to explain over the years. But lots of families had to do hard things to get by during the Depression. My uncle offered to take in the young son of his brother's widow to try to relieve her of some of the pressures of raising three children alone. My mother might have thought it would give a young child who had lost his father a fresh start under blue skies. What we soon realized was that we really needed to hold on to each other.

But Pyrites has a place in the list of the major influences on my life. It's where, looking back on it, I first saw that I could entertain total strangers with my singing. The parents at school didn't know me as a son, nephew, or cousin, just a little kid from New York City who could sing them a tune. I liked learning that and seeing the delight in their eyes. And I think even my uncle would agree that I've had a much better life singing than I would have had milking cows.

And I have Pyrites to thank for introducing me to nature. I loved the trees and the flowers and the grass rolling on for miles, not just the blocks by which we tended to measure the world back in Queens. What a work of art a tree is! The form, the colors, and the way it changes and grows. I see what looks like a lush, rolling ocean of trees from my windows overlooking Central Park today, but I first really saw the glory of trees in Pyrites.

And I fell in love with the river in winter: the beautiful, serene St. Lawrence River, which would freeze so thick and solid, it became a kind of glorious white avenue of ice. I learned how to skate there, and the frozen river would take me away. I'd skate mile after mile in the ice and sun, in the calm and quiet of the piles of soft snow along the riverbank and hanging in the trees, and I'd feel the peace of nature in my soul.

Golden Pavilion

7

Count Basie

I think Bill Basie was the greatest bandleader in American music. A bandleader is a different cat than a symphony conductor. A bandleader has to take a group of musicians who are soloists, by experience and temperament, and turn them into a band with one beating, swinging heart, while giving each of the players a featured turn.

It's art and it's chemistry. It's as if a baseball team had Babe Ruth, Joe DiMaggio, and Derek Jeter, but all at once. Sounds like an unbeatable lineup—but not if they can't be led into how to play together. And not if you can't tell Babe, "You still get to swing away."

Year after year, Bill Basie had Lester Young and Herschel Evans on sax, Buck Clayton and Harry "Sweets" Edison on trumpet, Jo Jones on drums, Benny Morton and Dicky Wells on trombone, and a roster of great singers that included Joe Williams, Helen Humes, and Billie Holiday. The Count's unique, wizardly touch was to blend those artists in a way that showcased each player's unique, extraordinary gifts.

Lester Young, who hung nicknames around people like prize medallions, called Bill Basie "Holy Man."

I guess I'd dreamed of working with Bill ever since I heard his "One O'Clock Jump" just before I went off to war. Then I came back, started singing in clubs, and saw COUNT BASIE AND HIS ORCHESTRA on one marquee after another up and down 52nd Street while I tried to break into the business. In 1958, I finally got my chance.

I was with Columbia Records, and Bill was with Roulette Records. I would need Columbia's approval to make a record with Bill, on his label or ours. Mitch Miller, with whom I had plenty of disagreements when he was head of Columbia, said, "What do you want to work with a junk label like Roulette for?"

The answer, of course, was that I'd do anything to work with Bill Basie.

But the companies which had us under contract couldn't have been more different.

Columbia was the class act of the recording industry. It was the label Frank Sinatra built. Mitch Miller lured Frankie Laine from Mercury and signed Doris Day, Rosemary Clooney, Johnny Mathis, the Four Lads, and, I'm pleased to say, me (and soon thereafter, the great Miles Davis). Columbia put out the Columbia Masterworks albums under Goddard Lieberson, which included all the great Broadway shows of the time (*West Side Story* and *My Fair Lady* became huge best sellers). It was the label of classical stars that included Leonard Bernstein, Eugene Ormandy, Glenn Gould, Aaron Copland, and Igor Stravinsky.

Columbia's engineers were the leading innovators of audio. They devised the LP, so you could play an entire movement of a symphony on one side (or, as with Columbia's 1946 *The Voice of Frank Sinatra*, a "concept album" of songs grouped around a theme). It transformed the recording industry artistically and commercially.

Columbia's 30th Street recording studio had once been a church, and it became regarded as holy ground for the recording industry. Glenn Gould recorded his *Goldberg Variations* there and Vladimir Horowitz his entire Masterworks discography. Miles Davis wouldn't record anywhere else.

Bill's label, Roulette Records, was another kind of story in the music business. A guy named Morris Levy founded the label as part of a front for the Genovese crime family (Morris would finally be convicted of extortion in 1986; he died before serving any time in prison). He did sign some great stars for Roulette, including Count Basie, Pearl Bailey, Ronnie Hawkins, and Dinah Washington and—I'll say this for him—gave them creative freedom.

But Morris Levy exploited his stars, including Bill Basie. He signed many of them to long-term contracts at low wages (when a company is mobbed up, any offer that lets you keep your neck sounds like a bargain) and hid their money behind intricate accounting tricks. Tommy James of Tommy James and the Shondells said Morris Levy bilked their group out of at least $30 million.

Bill Basie liked to gamble. But Morris didn't try to get him help; he just got him in deeper. He paid off Bill's debts to gamblers, who were usually also mobbed up, and in exchange put Bill on Roulette's payroll. Bill told me that he never earned any royalties from all those great albums he recorded for Roulette, just small checks from the company store.

Comparing Columbia to Roulette was a little like the *New Yorker* trying to put out an issue with a scandal sheet.

Bill and I decided to record two albums together, one for each record label. Mitch Miller was aghast and kept refusing to authorize the project. But I kept asking. Mitch had a new hit record out—"The Yellow Rose of Texas"—that was also in the classic film *Giant*. The week it replaced "Rock Around the Clock" as the number one hit, I decided it would be a good time to ask again. Mitch would be likely to be in a good mood.

"Go ahead," he told me. "If you want to ruin your career." Maybe he was even hoping for that.

Bill Basie and I had spoken only on the phone. But when we finally met in a rehearsal studio, joined by his great band, there were mutual respect and electricity. We ran through a couple of numbers, and Bill turned to those great musicians and pointed at me.

"Give this man anything he wants," he said.

Our first recording was a live album for Columbia, recorded at the Latin Casino in Philadelphia in November 1958. It was a great room, but small. The engineers had to set up the recording console in the basement kitchen.

The recording captured the night. We had a superb collection of talents who had fun, and tried to take songs we loved to new heights. Ralph Sharon joined us on piano, and we made great versions of "Just in Time," "Lost in the Stars," and "Fascinating Rhythm." The recording had crackle, sizzle, and spontaneity.

But then Columbia executives got hold of it. Stereo recording had just been developed, and Columbia wanted to show that the company was at the leading edge of technology. So the next month, they brought Bill and his band, Ralph Sharon, and me into a snug, quiet studio, where we rerecorded every single track. Later they added the crowd reaction and applause from the original Latin Casino recording to try to make the whole mixed-up bag sound "live."

Instead, it sounded like a dud. They were using great musicians and the latest technology to try to fool people. I thought the album, which they called *In Person!*, fooled no one into thinking that it worked. I thought it was in bad taste.

Bill and I went into the Capitol studios in New York just a month later to record our album for Roulette. This one is much more to my liking. It was called *Count Basie/Tony Bennett: Strike Up the Band*, named after our opening Gershwin tune, but Morris Levy licensed the recording to so many people over the years that it's reappeared under countless titles.

Bill's respect for my singing helped establish me with jazz lovers and cemented an enduring friendship. He had a sly, warm sense of humor. We appeared at the White House in 1963, and during a reception we both noticed the thick, sumptuous green drapes with gold tassels. Bill lifted one of the small gold balls hanging from a tassel and muttered to me, "My tax dollars paid for this?"

Another time we played the Academy of Music in Philadelphia and the appearance was phenomenal—ten standing ovations. But Bill and I were out in the parking lot after the performance when a white man tossed him his car keys.

"Hey, buddy," he said to Count Basie, "get my car, will you?"

I'm not sure how I would have reacted in Bill's shoes. Would any white man? But Count Basie was a bandleader. He knew how to kid, cajole, and josh people his way.

"Get your own car, buddy," he told the man. "I'm tired, I've been parking them all night."

It was the response of a genius. The guy got his car, and the Count kept his nobility. The man never knew what a fool he was.

Bill Basie taught me how to pace a show. I'd often open with a showstopping kind of a number to get everyone on their feet, stomping and clapping.

But Bill asked, "Why open with a closer?" He thought a show could only go downhill from there.

"Start with a medium-tempo number like 'Just in Time,'" he suggested, "and give the audiences a chance to settle in."

Most of all, I think Count Basie showed me the value of sticking to your artistic convictions.

The era of big band music was supposed to be over at the end of World War II, and Bill disbanded his orchestra. But it was back as a sixteen-piece orchestra by the early 1950s. The era of big band music may have passed. But Count Basie's sound and talents were in high demand, and he became the first choice of great vocalists, including Frank and Ella.

I talked to Bill during some of my most challenging years at Columbia. Clive Davis, a corporate attorney and very bright man, had been the head of business affairs at the label, and became president in 1967. He was the first guy from the business side to be appointed head of the label, and Clive's ascension marked the moment that the businesspeople in the recording industry began to take control from the creative people. It would happen at label after label.

Clive went to the 1967 Monterey Pop Festival. He came back wearing love beads and brandishing contracts with a bunch of new artists, including Janis Joplin and Big Brother and the Holding Company.

Clive had a sharp eye for talent (he would soon also sign Chicago, Billy Joel, Blood, Sweat & Tears, Pink Floyd, and Bruce Springsteen) and a hard head for business. He was convinced, with the ardency of a recent convert, that only rock music would sell in the '60s and '70s.

My records did well and made a lot of money for Columbia. I recorded Ron Miller and Orland Murden's fabulous song "For Once in My Life" in 1967, and it was the first time that great

Motown song hit the pop charts (although I'll be the first to admit that Stevie Wonder's 1968 recording has made it a Stevie Wonder song for a lot of people, and I was delighted that we could record a slower ballad version together on *Duets: An American Classic* in 2006). I had another enduring hit the next year with my album *Yesterday I Heard the Rain*, which led off with that great song by the same name by Gene Lees and Armando Manzanero.

But Clive thought my refusal to record rock and pop hits kept me (and the label) from making more money. He told me I was "looking over my shoulder musically," not keeping pace. He gave similar speeches to Peggy Lee, Lena Horne, and Mel Tormé.

Imagine telling Peggy Lee that she was "looking over her shoulder musically"!

I groused about some of those artistic stresses and regrets with Bill Basie. He also felt some of those pressures but generally resisted them. The kind of music we did had art, story, and style, he said. It moved and reached people. Thousands of people still turned out to hear his orchestra and buy his albums. Why try to be trendy when you can be timeless?

Or as Count Bill Basie asked me and I have since so often reminded myself, "Why change an apple?"

Still Life, New York, 1970

8

Judy Garland

J udy Garland was the little girl who made everybody happy but herself. When she came out onstage—small as a wounded bird but with that huge, gorgeous voice that reached the back of the house—everyone wanted to take care of her. Nobody in show business was more loved than Judy Garland, and sometimes it seemed that everyone but Judy knew that.

I had been her fan since I was a boy and she was a child star on the silver screen, so vivacious, wholesome, and gloriously talented. Nobody threw her heart into a song like Judy Garland. You could hear her heart beat and quiver with every note.

She came backstage to meet me after one of my shows at the Ambassador Hotel in Los Angeles in 1958. To be told "Judy Garland wants to say hello" was like hearing that a shooting star wanted to stop by.

The Judy I knew in person was rarely like a wounded bird. She bubbled. She dazzled and joked with a wicked sense of humor that would have made young Dorothy and her pal the Scarecrow blush.

It's funny that the woman who charmed so many childhoods never really had a childhood of her own. She was performing with her sisters in a vaudeville act (the Gumm Sisters, before they changed the name to Garland) before Judy was three years old. She had not only talent but star power—that hard-to-define quality that makes people want to look at you. It made her career but didn't always leave much over for her life.

Judy was thirteen when she sang "Zing! Went the Strings of My Heart" at an audition and signed what amounted to a development contract by Metro-Goldwyn-Mayer. She sang "You Made Me Love You" to Clark Gable at his studio birthday party and made such a strong impression that they wrote a scene for her to reprise the tune, singing to Clark's smiling photograph, in *Broadway Melody of 1938*.

Judy became one of MGM's biggest stars in the five films she made with Mickey Rooney, even before *The Wizard of Oz*. But she never felt that the studio protected her as the extraordinary asset she was. She made a dozen films in three years, including the Andy Hardy films with Mickey, *The Wizard of Oz*, and Busby Berkeley's *Babes in Arms* (she started shooting *Babes* just after *Wizard*; these days that would be like a star athlete going from one Super Bowl season to the next without rest).

Imagine all the songs and dances she introduced in those films; then try to reckon up all of the rehearsals and early calls that went into achieving Judy's special level of perfection. Then add the five shows a day to promote the films in more than twenty cities across the country. It's a formula for exhaustion, stress, and killing pressure.

It was during that time, Judy always said, that she began to take drugs to go to sleep and drugs to wake up. As she got a little older, she added drinking to relax. Mickey Rooney, who loved her and tried to protect her many times, said that the MGM executives didn't get her started on that road. But I don't think a kid working twelve hours a day in major studio productions enters that downward cycle all on her own.

For all the adoration she received, Judy was insecure. She was not even five feet tall and was on the same lot as other glamorous young stars, such as Lana Turner, Elizabeth Taylor, and Ava Gardner. The studio toyed with Judy's appearance so much, she was made to feel ugly and unappreciated. Louis B. Mayer supposedly called her "the little hunchback," but he still relied on Judy to carry some of his biggest productions.

Judy never saw the money she made. It went directly to others, and she had little idea of what a success she had created for herself. I went backstage at one of her stage shows and told the promoter, as a nice gesture, to pay Judy in cash that night. I went to her dressing room after the show and found her playing with the money like a kid with a board game. She jumped onto her couch and spilled the bills over her head, over and over.

"Tony, look!" she exclaimed. "For the first time in my life, I've got money!"

One night, a few years later, I was about to go onstage at the Waldorf-Astoria when the stage manager stopped me. I knew it had to be important. He held out a phone. "It's Judy Garland," he said.

Her famous voice was rushed and strained. "Tony, I'm in my room at the St. Regis. There's a man here, and he's beating me up."

Some people would have called the cops. I went one better: I called Frank Sinatra. I knew Frank was at the Fontainebleau in Miami, and the moment I stepped offstage, the stage manager held out the phone. I was glad to hear Judy's voice. She was almost giggling.

"I wanted help, but this is ridiculous!" she said. "There are nine hundred cops downstairs and five lawyers in my room."

(The story never made it into the papers. Unthinkable today.)

Judy should have made more movies. She should have won the 1954 Oscar for Best Actress for *A Star Is Born*, which is one of the great musical and dramatic performances of all time (Grace Kelly won for *The Country Girl*—a fine performance, but watch them both and cast your vote), and maybe another Oscar for Best Supporting Actress in 1961 for *Judgment at Nuremberg*, where she steals the show in a courtroom cameo.

But Judy's troubles took a toll—on herself, of course, most of all—on producers, directors, and other actors in her films, and she lost out on a lot of work.

Her love of live performance endured, though, and the more the world heard of her problems, illnesses, and busted romances, the more people wanted to see her, embrace her, and cheer for her. The more they wanted to help Judy reach a safe place somewhere over the rainbow.

Her appearance at Carnegie Hall on the night of April 23, 1961, has been called the greatest night in the history of show business. I wouldn't want to disagree. Judy pulled some magic powers from all of her troubles and delivered a historic performance. The double album of that night won four Grammy Awards, was on the Billboard charts for seventy-three weeks, and has never been out of print since. Every song in the show seemed to resonate brilliantly with her career and life. In the space of an amazing two hours, she was the innocent young Judy of "The Trolley Song" and "Over the Rainbow," the wounded and weary Judy of "The Man That Got Away" and "Stormy Weather," and the dauntless, resilient Judy of "When

You're Smiling (The Whole World Smiles with You)." That night, it sure did.

Judy had a gorgeous contralto voice, and she packed feeling into every note. She told me once that it was a good idea to put at least one number into a show that lets you hit the back of the house with your voice—it makes everyone feel that they've somehow met you.

No performer was ever closer to her fans, and they ached for her when she asked, so famously, "If I am a legend, then why am I so lonely?"

I last saw Judy in London, in April 1969. I was doing a television special with Count Basie, and she came backstage.

"You know what, Tony?" she said. "You're pretty good."

We lost her just two months later, much too young, at the age of forty-seven. Of course it was tragic. But like the great performer she was, Judy Garland always left us wanting more.

Golden Gate Bridge

9

San Francisco

To tell you the truth, I had barely seen a cable car when I first sang that song.

Ralph Sharon, my longtime friend and piano player, found the sheet music to "I Left My Heart in San Francisco" in his shirt drawer, and it's affected the entire course of my life.

One day in the early 1950s, Ralph was walking down Broadway and ran into George Cory and Douglass Cross, two hopeful songwriters he sort of knew. They handed him a whole sheaf of their songs, which is what songwriters had to do before YouTube and Facebook.

Ralph was a gentleman and said he'd take a look. But we were constantly on tour, and he never had the chance. Until one day in late 1961 when he was packing for a western swing we were about to make that would take us to Hot Springs, Arkansas, then to San Francisco. Ralph opened his shirt drawer, moved a few things around, and noticed "I Left My Heart in San Francisco" on top. He took it along.

We played a great old place in Hot Springs called the Vapors Restaurant (Bill Clinton told me years later that he had stood outside the club—he was too young to get in—and watched our show through the window). One night after our show, Ralph was going over the material we wanted to perform in San Francisco and took out the song he'd found mixed up with his shirts. He got a few lines in and decided it had promise. He called me in my room. We met at the hotel bar, where there was a piano. Ralph began to pick out the tune and I began to sing, "High on a hill, it calls to me . . ."

I reached the last line, and the bartender who was setting up his station called us over. "If you guys record that song," he said, "I'll buy the first copy."

It would be the first of I don't know how many millions of copies that have been sold by now. Quite a few great singers— Frank Sinatra, Peggy Lee, Julie London, and Bobby Womack— have recorded it, too, but I don't mind saying: that's my song.

It went gold and won the Grammy for Record of the Year and the Grammy for Best Solo Vocal Performance, Male. "I Left My Heart in San Francisco" is ranked 23rd on the National Endowment of the Arts list of the most historically significant songs of the twentieth century and I don't know how many times I've sung it in stadiums for the San Francisco 49ers and San Francisco Giants (they both get into a lot of championship games). I sang it at the 50th anniversary celebration of the Golden Gate Bridge and when the San Francisco–Oakland Bay Bridge was reopened after the 1989 Loma Prieta earthquake. They play it in the ballpark every time the Giants—*my* Giants, I think I've earned the right to say—win a game.

People still ask me, "Do you ever get tired of singing it?" I ask them, "Do you ever get tired of making love?"

And the song wasn't even written for me.

This great song was written for Claramae Turner, an opera singer who began her career with the San Francisco Opera, and sang a fine version of "You'll Never Walk Alone" in the film *Carousel*. Claramae joined the Metropolitan Opera in New York but missed her hometown. George and Douglass, who were also from the Bay Area, were trying to make it in New York by then and, in a way, wrote the song for all three of them.

"It was pure nostalgia," George Cory said. "We missed the warmth and openness of the people and the beauty. We never really took to New York."

Claramae would often sing it as an encore for her recitals. But she never recorded the song commercially (you can hear a recorded version, just Claramae and an unidentified pianist, on the San Francisco Opera website).

Ralph and I performed it during our December 1961 show in the Venetian Room of the Fairmont Hotel. Audiences loved it, and word spread all over town. A local Columbia rep heard us in rehearsal and called New York to say we should record it, because the sales in San Francisco alone would be worthwhile.

Ralph and I went into the studio when we got back to New York in January and recorded the song in just one take. But it wound up on the B side of the single of "Once Upon a Time," a beautiful song by Charles Strouse and Lee Adams, from the musical *All American*.

But as DJ after DJ told us, people kept flipping over the record.

What makes "I Left My Heart in San Francisco" the great and enduring song that it is, more than fifty years after it was recorded?

There's that dreamy melody by George Cory, of course. Like

a lot of the best love songs, too, it's written out of longing and loneliness. And Doug's lyrics are terrific. They tell a story but let your mind and heart fill in the blanks.

"I've been terribly alone and forgotten in Manhattan . . ." Who hasn't felt forgotten in a strange city? "To be where little cable cars climb halfway to the stars . . ." is such a beguiling image to climb into. "The morning fog may chill the air, I don't care . . ."

And the line "My love waits there in San Francisco . . ." is songwriting brilliance. It touches your heart. Is it an old love you left behind? A new love you hope to find? A great song will let you put yourself inside it, to answer those questions for yourself, different answers for different times of your life

George and Doug once said that they almost made the song "When I Return to San Francisco." I don't know how Ralph and I would have reacted to that. "When I Return to San Francisco" sounds a little like you're reading an airplane ticket. "I Left My Heart"—you feel the love and longing, don't you?

The success of that song has steered the rest of my career. That record gave me a song with which I've been identified and, quite happily, always will be. "I Left My Heart in San Francisco" was my "Hound Dog," my "My Way," my "I Want to Hold Your Hand." It sent my career to another level. To this day, if I'm performing in Tallahassee or Tokyo, I know that's the song the audience is waiting to hear. I don't want to send them home disappointed.

It's also a good lesson: you never know what treasures might be packed away in the shirt drawer. It was a great song, just waiting to be discovered, and I'm glad Ralph Sharon did.

George and Doug, by the way, never had to write another song. They went back home to the Bay Area and built a beautiful mansion for themselves, although Douglass died, far too young, at the age of fifty-four in 1975. Ralph and I visited them a couple of times. They had letters from people all over the world, thanking them for their song. "I Left My Heart in San Francisco" changed my life and theirs, but I'm happy to say that it's touched the lives of a lot of other people, too. I was also thrilled in August 2016, when the Fairmont Hotel put a statue of me on their grounds.

I love being in San Francisco now, though it's hard for me to walk out on the street there without someone stopping me to sing me my own song—as if I hadn't heard it! But most of all, I love how I've become a part of that elegant, beautiful city that's a golden spot for people all over the world.

Den Bosch, Holland

Harold Arlen

Composers are a special breed of artist. They create the songs we walk around with in our heads for all of our lives. But how do they know what particular notes to put next to each other that will bring a tear or a smile, or make the skin on our arms stand on end?

I've been blessed to sing songs composed by some of the greatest composers in pop music (though I'm not going to list them here and risk leaving out a couple). But I've got to say I have a special place in my heart for Harold Arlen. His songs were unique and unconventional—almost like plays that swung among joy, regret, resignation, and celebration in just two to three minutes.

Singers admire Harold's compositions but approach them with caution. Many of his most popular songs have big leaps between notes that can challenge a performer. There's no better example than Harold's "Over the Rainbow." The very first two notes jump a full octave, from middle C to the C above middle

C. I'm sure there are music teachers out there who tell their students not to do that to a singer—or a song.

But "Over the Rainbow" has been ranked as the Song of the Century in a poll by the National Endowment of the Arts and is widely considered the greatest movie song of all time.

(Yip Harburg, one of Harold's best creative partners, wrote the haunting lyrics. In 1939, Harold and Yip also wrote "Lydia, the Tattooed Lady" for Groucho Marx, which may be the funniest song of all time. That's range!)

The Harold Arlen I knew was a dapper gent, who always wore a fresh flower in his lapel. He had a beautifully groomed mustache that gave him a dash of Errol Flynn. He was the son of a cantor from Buffalo, New York (his name at birth was Hyman Arluck; Arlen came from Orlin, his mother's maiden name), and was fascinated by blues and jazz from an early age. Harold could also sing and play a superb piano, and he toured with his own group for much of his twenties, then began to write shows for the famous Cotton Club in Harlem. His lyric writing partner then was Ted Koehler, and they created scores of gorgeous songs that are standards today, including "Stormy Weather" (the great Ethel Waters cut the first recording, and it's still a classic) and "Let's Fall in Love."

Love is what brought Harold to Hollywood in the 1930s. He married a stunning model and starlet named Anya Taranda, who was one of the original Breck Shampoo girls, and they were devoted to each other. But their marriage was not an easy melody. Anya had mental and emotional problems and had to be institutionalized for seven years. I've always wondered how that experience might have deepened Harold, and inflected some of his best-known songs with a touch of his own blues.

It was in Hollywood that he teamed up with Yip Harburg.

I've heard a couple of different versions of how they came up with "Over the Rainbow" in 1936, including one that says Harold saw a rainbow over Schwab's drugstore. In other interviews, he just said he was on a drive with Anya when the first notes came to him. But remember, *The Wizard of Oz* had several popular songs, including "If I Only Had a Brain" (Ray Bolger's Scarecrow) or "a Heart" (Jack Haley's Tin Man) or "the Nerve" (Bert Lahr's Cowardly Lion—maybe I ought to say "Da Noive") and "We're Off to See the Wizard." Harold and Yip were on staff at MGM, so they received no royalties.

In the 1940s, Harold started songwriting with Johnny Mercer, the great lyricist, and they produced one classic after another, including "Blues in the Night," "That Old Black Magic," "Come Rain or Come Shine," and "One for My Baby." And in the 1950s, Harold teamed with Ira Gershwin to write "The Man That Got Away" for Judy Garland in *A Star Is Born*.

So Harold Arlen wrote Judy Garland's signature songs both when she was young and when she was mature, and they happen to be perhaps the two greatest movie songs of all time. That's a good life's work, all by itself.

I loved Harold's song "So Long, Big Time!" and wanted to record it for my 1964 album *The Many Moods of Tony*. I was honored when Harold came to the recording session. That was rare for him. But "So Long, Big Time!" was a brand-new song. It had a wonderful lyric by Dorothy Langdon (later known as Dory Previn), the story of a man who was once up and is now down. "So long, so long / Big time / Big dough, bright lights / Big time."

We were excited to see Harold behind the control room glass, elegant with his fresh flower in his lapel, and wanted to do our best by his song. A lot of songwriters, for reasons I respect, don't want you to tinker with what they've written. They work hard to put every note and word into place, and their work deserves to be treated with deference.

But Harold didn't mind improvisation. He'd actually become enthusiastic about changes we would try from take to take, telling us "Hey, change it any way you like, as long as it works." In fact, Harold himself had suggestions about certain words I should hit, such as emphasizing the rhyme in "It was *fun* / Now it's *done*."

Maroon Bells

Harold was secure as an artist. He knew that there was something so identifiable at the core of his songs that he didn't worry about changes. He understood, as artists must, that you roll what you create into the world, and then it flies away on its own. The world takes over from there. His example helped me see that I should enjoy and treasure collaboration. Nobody has all the best ideas, and working with others helps keep you fresh and invigorated. That's how Harold wrote all those great songs year after year, decade after decade.

São Paulo, Brazil

Harry Belafonte

In the late '40s, there was a group of us—singers (including Barbara Carroll, my dear friend to this day), comics, and actors, all trying to snag jobs—who hung out at Hanson's Drug Store on 52nd Street, slurping coffee, sipping milk shakes, and trying to figure out who would really make it in the business. You've heard of some of the names we knew and talked about. You haven't heard about a lot more. We'd go through a list of pros and cons: "Good voice. Small personality. Wrong material. Not unless . . ."

But whenever Harry Belafonte's name came up, the answer was immediate and emphatic: "Sure thing. No doubt. That classic profile. That dusky voice. That charm and grace . . ." We'd shake our heads in envy and go back to our milk shakes.

Harry Belafonte became one of the most successful and beloved entertainers in America, from the 1950s until now, really. He made folk music sexy. He made traditional tunes from all around the world into big hits in the United States.

(Almost everyone knows at least "Day-o!" from "Banana Boat Song," but have you ever heard his "Hava Nagila"? I wonder how many Jewish kids learned the song from listening to Harry's record.)

But he also showed us how to take the fame we've been lucky enough to earn and use it to try to make life better for others. Harry did so in countless ways. Some of what he's done got a lot of publicity. But a lot only a few people know. Harry Belafonte has shown us how a star can also be a source for change.

Harry was born in Harlem's famous Lying-in Hospital, the year after I was born in Astoria. He had a mixed-race background, including a Dutch grandfather who was a Sephardic Jew. He was sent off to live with his grandmother in Jamaica for much of his childhood. He returned to New York for high school, served in the US Navy when it was still segregated, and fell in love when a resident in the building where he was a janitor's assistant gave him tickets to the American Negro Theatre as a tip. Harry saw live theater and knew he wanted to be a performer.

He started taking drama classes at the New School, and was classmates with the incredible Sidney Poitier. I love Harry's story that he and Sidney were so poor, they'd buy a single ticket to the theater and hand it off during intermission, the one who had seen the first half filling in the other one about what happened.

Harry began to sing in clubs around town to pay for his drama classes. He sang pop and jazz first, before settling on the folk music that he loved and believed in. It made him famous around the world: "Matilda," "Banana Boat Song," and "Jamaica Farewell" were all huge best sellers that are now considered classics.

Harry succeeded—both in show business and in real life—by being true to his convictions.

Harry was the first person I can remember who told me about Dr. Martin Luther King, Jr. Harry had heard him preach at the esteemed Abyssinian Baptist Church in Harlem and felt that his message should resound around the country. He was an early contributor to Dr. King's Southern Christian Leadership Conference and helped draw support for the SCLC from many show business figures, including Marlon Brando, Eartha Kitt, and, it's sometimes forgotten, Charlton Heston.

Dr. King was on tour at a department store in Harlem in the fall of 1958 when a proper-looking woman approached him at the desk where he was signing books and said, "I've been looking for you for five years." Izola Ware Curry, an African American woman who was originally from Georgia, plunged a seven-inch-long, ivory-handled steel letter opener into Dr. King's chest.

A seven-hour-long operation saved Dr. King's life, but the tip of the blade had been so close to his aorta, the doctors told him that if he sneezed, he would die. Harry went to see him in the hospital and made sure Dr. King's wife and infant son could come up from Montgomery, Alabama, to join him. It was during those tense, dramatic days that Martin told Harry that his one overriding fear about dying was that no one would be there to care for his young son, Martin III.

Harry's response was instinctive, generous, and practical.

"The work you do for all of us is so important," he told Dr. King, "I never want you to worry about providing for your children. I never want you to have to do something for the money. I'll take care of everything."

Quietly and with little notice, Harry established a trust fund that eventually paid for the schooling of Martin and Coretta Scott King's four children. There is no tax break for that kind of generosity, or even a plaque on a building. But it enabled Dr. King to go about the United States and do the work that made us a better country.

Harry's enormous popularity interested the film studios, and he starred in a few projects that tried to take advantage of his extraordinary good looks and magnetic presence. The best remembered may be *Carmen Jones*, the musical he made with the great Dorothy Dandridge (incredibly, although both Dorothy and Harry were famous singers, their songs in the films were dubbed by opera singers, Marilyn Horne for Dorothy, Lavern Hutcherson for Harry), and 1959's *The World, the Flesh, and the Devil*, an interesting little science fiction film with Inger Stevens in which a black man and a white woman are the only visible survivors of a nuclear war.

Harry was offered the chance to costar with Dorothy again in Otto Preminger's film of *Porgy and Bess*. But Harry didn't like the stereotypes he felt the film portrayed and he turned the film down flat. His good friend Sidney Poitier ended up playing the role, but only under protest (Preminger threatened to sue Sidney because his agent had given him an oral agreement). Harry was disenchanted with Hollywood—actually, he was never really enchanted—and went back to music. He wouldn't make films for years (though he later won many awards for his appearance in Robert Altman's 1996 Jazz Age drama, *Kansas City*).

While Harry toured and made television specials, he continued his career as a social activist, both publicly and quietly. When Dr. King was arrested in 1963 and put into the Birmingham city jail, Harry paid his bail and that of many other protesters. As Harry says, "You can cage the singer, but not the song." He helped fund and organize the Freedom Rides and the 1963 March on Washington. He more or less financed the

Student Nonviolent Coordinating Committee in its early days during the Mississippi Freedom Summer of 1964.

So when Harry called me in the spring of 1965 to say he wanted me to join Dr. King's march in Selma, I felt that I couldn't say no. Harry had done so much already that walking a few miles along a highway was the very least I could do.

To me, Harry is the model of a man who has steered his life by his convictions, both personally and professionally. He has won Grammy and Emmy awards, traveled around the world and brought back great talents, including Nana Mouskouri and Miriam Makeba, and introduced them to American audiences. But he has also given time and commitment (not just money, like many stars) to causes that include the antiapartheid movement, civil rights, and juvenile justice. He has made his social and political convictions his work, as much as he has his music.

Harry Belafonte has shown us not to wait in life to work for what you believe in. Make it part of your life, each and every day.

Night Scene, Manila

Martin Luther King, Jr.

One of the most treasured photos that I keep in my office shows my friend Harry Belafonte and me smiling on either side of his friend Dr. Martin Luther King, Jr. The picture was snapped backstage at Carnegie Hall in January 1961 at a tribute to Dr. King to benefit his Southern Christian Leadership Conference (Count Basie was also there, along with Frank Sinatra, Dean Martin, Sammy Davis, Jr., Mahalia Jackson, Carmen McRae, Buddy Hackett, and many more stars of the caliber that only a great cause—and Harry Belafonte—could bring together).

Anyone can look at himself in an old photo and reflect, "How young I was." But I look at that photo and realize that Dr. King was just thirty-two, a couple of years younger than Harry and me. Yet he was already an international hero for his amazing oratory and boundless courage in leading countless civil rights campaigns and demonstrations.

He was gracious to all of us backstage and carried himself with such dignity and princely bearing that you knew you were in the presence of someone who was a great soul. It's a little startling to look at that photo and realize how much a man who was barely into his thirties had already shaken history and inspired the world.

I owe a lot to Dr. Martin Luther King. Every American does.

If they have room for another bust on Mount Rushmore, it should be of Dr. King. Not only did he give his life for equal rights for all Americans, he showed us how to return hatred with love. He was Gandhi's message of peace and nonviolence in a walking, breathing, brave human being.

But those of us in the music business owe a special debt to Dr. King and the civil rights revolution that he and others brought about with such great effort and cost. We knew the genius of so many African Americans firsthand: it was in the music we performed every day. We would not have had our careers—our lives—without the gifts of the African American artists who created jazz and the blues, our great American musical art forms.

We also knew that for a long time, a lot of our greatest musical geniuses—Duke Ellington, Louis Armstrong, Ella Fitzgerald, Billie Holiday, Nat "King" Cole, as well as millions of other people—could not even sit at the same table we did in a restaurant. I don't know how many times I'd come to see Nat or Ella perform in a supper club where they would bring in hundreds of people but couldn't walk in through the same door or be a customer. America was crazy.

Martin Luther King electrified me when I first saw him on grainy black-and-white news film in the late 1950s. You could glimpse the majesty of his character, even in short clips. And there was a powerful musicality in his speeches, with his great voice pealing like a golden trumpet as he asked a crowd how long their struggle would last.

"How long? Not long! Because no lie can live forever. How long? Not long! Because 'you shall reap what you sow,'" and the crowd coming back with "Yes sir, Doctor." "How long? Not long! Because the arc of the moral universe is long, but it bends toward justice . . ."

Harry Belafonte called me in March 1965. Dr. King and his lieutenants had been organizing and leading peaceful marches and protests to assert the right of blacks to register to vote. After a rally in late February, a twenty-six-year-old church deacon named Jimmie Lee Jackson had been clubbed and shot to death by Alabama state troopers (the trooper who pulled the trigger, James Bonard Fowler, wouldn't be indicted until 2007 and pleaded guilty to second-degree manslaughter, serving just five months in prison for the death of an innocent man).

Reverend James Bevel of Dr. King's Southern Christian Leadership Conference mapped out three long marches, fifty-four miles, from Selma to the state capitol in Montgomery, Alabama. The first march, on March 7, 1965, became known as Bloody Sunday after state troopers attacked the marchers with tear gas and billy clubs. Dr. King himself led the next march, on March 9; to avoid a confrontation, he just led the group back to a church. But that night, a group of white thugs beat and killed the Reverend James Reeb, a minister from Boston who had joined the march (four men would be indicted for his death, but three were acquitted by all-white juries, and the fourth fled to Mississippi and never stood trial).

The third march was set for March 21, 1965. "We need you, Tony," Harry said when he reached me. "People are being slaughtered all over Alabama."

The governor of Alabama, George Wallace, refused to protect the marchers. So President Lyndon Johnson said he would federalize the Alabama National Guard and send two thousand US Army soldiers and an army of federal marshals and FBI agents to Alabama.

"I hate violence, Harry," I told him. "I saw too much of it during the war."

"That's why we need you, Tony," he told me. "To try to stop the violence."

So I went down to Selma for the third and final march. Dr. King and Harry had also persuaded some other performers, including Sammy Davis, Jr., Shelley Winters, Betty Comden and Adolph Green, and Leonard Bernstein, to join the march. I roomed with my old friend Billy Eckstine, the great deep-voiced, and drop-dead-handsome singer, and we joined people from all over the country to march ten miles a day along what was then called in Alabama the Jefferson Davis Highway.

It was thrilling and inspiring to march. But also a little frightening—more than a little. The state troopers cursed and spat along the route, and tapped their guns and billy clubs. Everyone knew that blood had already been shed. I hadn't been so frightened since my days in a foxhole in Germany. But Alabama was supposed to be in the United States of America.

One night, Dr. King asked us performers to put on a show. It was the least we could do for such brave people. No stage was available—the state troopers wouldn't permit an integrated group to perform in a theater or school along the route—so someone called a nearby funeral home. A local mortician rolled out his inventory. We did a show on top of eighteen wooden caskets that became our stage. I sang a few numbers, but the only song I really remember is "Just in Time," which now seems kind of oddly appropriate.

Both Billy and I had previous engagements that couldn't be

canceled and we had to leave before the march ended in Montgomery. We must have been a little jumpy and distracted when we packed, because a few days later, Billy called me in New York from Los Angeles.

"Tony," he said in that deep, mellifluous voice that had made such hits of "Blue Moon" and "Sophisticated Lady," "where are my damn pants?" Billy was six foot two, I was five foot nine, but we had packed each other's pants and been too nervous to notice.

Yet the full impact of events wouldn't strike us until a few days later. Billy and I had been given a lift to the airport by a mother of five from Detroit, who told us she had heard Martin Luther King, Jr., say that the struggle for equal rights going on in Alabama was for all Americans. So she had driven down to Selma to try to help. Because she had a '63 Oldsmobile (and probably because she was white and less likely to be stopped by state troopers), Viola Liuzzo was assigned to ferry supplies between the march sites and many of the volunteers arriving from all over the country.

I wish I could tell you that I remember our conversation when she drove Billy and me to the Montgomery airport. I just remember admiring this bold, appealing woman—a mother of five kids who was putting herself on the line for civil rights.

Billy and I played our gigs and picked up our lives in show business. Meanwhile, Viola Liuzzo stayed on to see the great Selma-to-Montgomery march finally reach the end on March 25, 1965. A Confederate flag flew over the state capitol, but Martin Luther King told the crowd, "Our aim must never be to defeat or humiliate the white man, but to win his friendship and understanding. We must come to see that the end we seek is a society at peace with itself, a society that can live with its conscience. And that will be a day not of the white man, not of the black man. That will be the day of man as man."

What magnificence of soul and spirit for a man who had been stung so much by the lash of segregation.

After the march, Viola and another volunteer, a nineteen-year-old named Leroy Moton, drove some of the marchers back to Selma. They had turned around to head back to Montgomery and were stopped at a red light when four white men—Ku Klux Klan members—pulled up alongside and began to follow them. Viola Liuzzo tried to outrun them, but the men waited for a remote stretch of highway and opened fire.

They murdered Viola Liuzzo, a courageous mother of five from Detroit who gave her life for civil rights. She was only thirty-nine years old—the same age as Martin Luther King when he was assassinated just three years later.

My personal contact with Martin Luther King, Jr., was limited. But his struggle, his achievements, and his living embodiment of the power of love continue to inspire me and millions more. I am as proud (more proud, really, in many ways) to have been a small part, with so many others, of his march from Selma to Montgomery as I am of any Grammy Award or gold record.

We still have a lot of work to do on racial equality in America. We still have a lot of work to do to instill peace. But Dr. King's great gift to us all was to show us that there's a path to a better way if we're bold enough to take it. In my own small way, I try to use my art, my music, and the work we have done in schools to try to help move us along a little more on the path Dr. King so nobly set. He inspires me every day, as much as do the greatest composers and artists. Martin Luther King's life ended too soon, but it is timeless.

Miyamoto Musashi: Shrike

Carmel Highlands, California

Fred Astaire

red Astaire used to float past my house on his morning walk when I lived in Beverly Hills in the 1970s. That's the only way to say it—Fred just didn't move like anyone else. He would be only going to mail a letter or get a sniff of air, but he had a special grace in the smallest, simplest gestures.

The Fred Astaire I got to know was friendly and sociable, but he avoided going to parties.

"Every woman in the room wants me to get up and dance with them, Tony," he told me. "I can't enjoy myself."

Fred was in his seventies by the time I became his neighbor and would take an occasional straight acting role or even record a song. But he said he had mostly given up dancing. We used to sit and talk in a small art studio I had in back of my house, and one day I had to slip into the main house to take a phone call. I had the radio tuned to a local jazz station. I returned to find the great Fred Astaire dancing to a Big Joe Turner tune. I felt blessed to be a solitary audience.

Fred practically blushed. "When I hear the right beat," he told me, "I still just *have* to dance."

By universal agreement, Fred was the greatest popular dancer of all time. But a lot of people don't appreciate what a fine singer he was, too, or how many classic songs he made famous in his films, including George and Ira Gershwin's "They Can't Take That Away from Me" in the 1937 movie *Shall We Dance*, Cole Porter's "Night and Day" from the 1932 film *The Gay Divorcee*, Jerome Kern and Dorothy Fields's "The Way You Look Tonight" in the 1936 film *Swing Time*, and Irving Berlin's "Cheek to Cheek" in *Top Hat* in 1935.

I could go on and on. I know that Frank Sinatra made "One for My Baby (and One More for the Road)" into his own personal theme song. But Fred actually sang that great Harold Arlen and Johnny Mercer song first, in the 1943 film *The Sky's the Limit*. It's worth finding the video clip today. When Fred sings, "Drop another nickel in the machine," he flips a coin onto the bar and it spins and spins like some whirling, magic top.

Only Fred Astaire could flip a nickel like that.

His voice was soft but fine, which was more important. He found the rhythm and feeling in a song, and put it across with elegance and grace. Every word counted. No wonder so many great songwriters wanted to write for Fred Astaire. He was such a standard of grace that the great Cole Porter had to put him ("the nimble tread of the feet of Fred Astaire") into the lyrics of "You're the Top."

I learned a lot from Fred about what I've come to think of as the clean line of elegance in art, whether it's painting, dance, or music. He choreographed so many of his famous dances with Hermes Pan and would rehearse them for weeks before he ever went before the cameras. Fred said he would begin by putting everything into a routine. Then each time he did it, he would discover, step-by-step, what he could leave out. "I make it perfect," he said, "then take out fifteen minutes."

Fred said that made his moves look effortless. I think you see the same idea in the clean, elegant lines of a Picasso sketch, and that's what I try to put into my songs. Learn what you don't really need, and leave it out.

Stardust, Las Vegas

Cary Grant

One of the reasons I moved to California for a few years was that I thought I should make more movies. No less than Cary Grant told me I was crazy.

I got to know Cary at a few parties. He was as charming, droll, and debonair—well, as Cary Grant. He saw one of my paintings, *South of France*, when I showed it to Johnny Carson on *The Tonight Show Starring Johnny Carson* and told me he wanted to buy it; he wouldn't take it as a gift. I was so proud when he hung it in his home in Hollywood Hills.

Cary and I were talking once, and I told him a little about my work life. He had retired from movies in the late 1960s, in part to spend more time with his young daughter, Jennifer, whom he cherished. But he also began to make occasional stage appearances around the country where he would show film clips and take questions from adoring audiences.

I told him how I'd have to fly across the country sometimes to do six shows in five days; it could take a toll. All the miles, all

Venice in '03

the hours, the exhaustion. Yes, I guess I was complaining. But Cary saw it differently.

"Tony, what you do is so beautiful," he said. "You can go out and meet people. Let me tell you, making movies is boring. You sit around for hours while somebody changes a lightbulb. You wait around all day in your trailer just to say three or four lines. It's lonely. It's dull. Stay with your music, Tony. You're so lucky to work, live, and to be able to see and talk to people. It's a blessing."

I suppose I already knew that. But when Cary Grant tells you something, it makes an impression. He influenced my decision to focus on live performances, where I can see the public, hear them, and not be isolated from them. It's why I still love to perform and tour more than sixty years later.

Cary, by the way, was preparing to go onstage at the Adler Theatre in Davenport, Iowa, for one of his shows in 1986 when he suffered the stroke that ended his life at the age of eighty-two. I remember people saying that they'd expected him to bid good-bye to this earth in Hollywood, Cannes, or Monaco—but Iowa?

Then I remembered how much he had told me he loved audiences. I think backstage in a theater in Iowa was probably just fine with Cary Grant.

Winter in Clio

Cole Porter

I have probably sung scores of Cole Porter's songs thousands of times, and each time it's like opening some exquisitely made treasure. All the internal rhymes and "clever entendres," like these special lines from "Let's Do It (Let's Fall in Love)":

In shallow shoals English soles do it
Goldfish in the privacy of bowls do it
Let's do it, let's fall in love.

Cole wrote that for *Paris*, the show that was his first Broadway success, in 1928. Looking back on it, a lot of factors were coming into play then that made Cole's music such a fitting accompaniment for the time. Recording technology and radio were beginning to make music an everyday companion in American homes. The talkies—motion pictures with sound!—were packing in millions of Americans who were eager to see and hear the musical talents they had heard about. And the microphone, which could not only project a voice but also isolate it, emphasized the value of wordplay and memorable lyrics to make a song popular.

Then add the Great Depression—that's an important part, too. Americans wanted entertainment, and Cole's songs reminded them of elegance and wit. His songs were a glass of bubbly in flat times.

We don't think of Cole as a jazz figure. But jazz artists loved to perform Cole Porter's songs. His lyrics demanded the best, most precise phrasing from a singer. And Cole's gift for concealing the risqué in the turn of an elegant phrase ("Why ask if shad do it? / Waiter, bring me shad roe") was a sly trick that jazz and blues performers had sought, too, and admired.

One of the favorite duets that I get to sing with the glorious Lady Gaga is Cole Porter's "Anything Goes." It's the title song of his 1934 musical (the great Ethel Merman first sang that song, and not a word was lost).

I sang this with Gaga on our 2014 album, *Cheek to Cheek*. Tom Lanier on piano and a host of great jazz artists accompanied us.

Gaga told me that she first remembered hearing the song when she was thirteen and immediately heard the fun in Cole's song. As she got older, she heard the powerful sexy vibe, too.

I'd recorded the song on my own a couple of times. But Gaga's excitement over joining forces for our own version of this classic Cole was contagious. We loved doing Cole's song in the studio and delight in singing it onstage today. We hand the lines back and forth because the way Cole composed the song and fit the lyrics inside of it makes it as irresistible as tossing a ball back and forth. The opposing rhymes and contrasting words bing back and forth in every line, then wind up interlocking like a Rubik's Cube:

And good's bad today,
And black's white today
And day's night today

Yet this man known for putting wit and cleverness into every line could also be sincerely simple and direct. So many of us have recorded Cole's song "I've Got You under My Skin." Virginia Bruce got to sing it first, in Cole's 1936 MGM musical *Born to Dance*. A lot of historians rank Frank Sinatra's 1946 recording as one of his signature songs. I think Dinah Washington and Diana Krall have recorded especially great takes on the song, too. It not only begins with a single, arresting image—I've got you under my skin—but stays with that image line after line, which is exactly what romantic love does, isn't it?

Yet again Cole found internal rhymes and quotable wordplay ("So deep in my heart that you're really a part of me").

I never met Cole Porter. His legs were crushed in a horse-riding accident in the late 1930s, and he lived for years with crippling pain. He had thirty-four operations over the years to try to save his legs and end his pain. By the time I began to make it in show business in the 1950s, one of Cole's legs had been amputated, and his wife had died. This man, known for living large (the story, which he encouraged, was that Cole had brought along his piano when he joined the French Foreign Legion after World War I) and giving glittering parties that included the most glamorous people of the times, was living more or less in isolation at the Waldorf. He was admired, beloved, but lonely. He died in southern California in 1964.

I don't know of any Cole Porter today. I don't mean that there aren't plenty of people who are writing clever, intricate, affecting songs that will live for a long time. But Cole was a kind of gold standard. His songs were universally acclaimed and enjoyed by all types of people, from classical music fans to jazz enthusiasts. His songs were unlike anyone else's, even as so many others tried to imitate him, consciously or unconsciously. Cole Porter's songs set a standard for American popular music and elevated it to new heights. He made the music we sing take off. He taught me that being original inspires others.

Foggy Day in Central Park

Central Park

16

Nat "King" Cole

Nat "King" Cole was the soul of elegance. He sang like an angel, played piano with precision and grace, and had a generosity that can be rare in any line of work.

But I never will forget (none of us should) that when I went to see him in his dressing room in a Miami club in the 1950s and invited him to join me at my table after the show, he just shook his head and smiled.

"Can't do that here, Tony," he told me. "I'll just have to see you in the dressing room."

What he meant, of course, was that Miami and the rest of the South (and practically speaking, some places in the North, too) were still segregated. The star of the show—the man whose name packed the house—couldn't sit at the same table as a customer because of the color of his skin.

I remember hearing Nat on a V-Disc when I was still a soldier in Germany. I didn't know his name then. But I couldn't forget how his soft, silky baritone conveyed such warmth and feeling or how his enunciation was so exact and elegant.

Scores of great singers have recorded "Mona Lisa," the wonderful song by Ray Evans and Jay Livingston; I certainly have. But say the words, and I'll bet most people think of Nat "King" Cole, maybe even more than they think of Leonardo da Vinci.

Nat told me once that his mother had been his only music teacher. He began with gospel in his Bronzeville neighborhood on the South Side of Chicago, but she insisted he learn Bach and Rachmaninoff, too. The South Side rocked with great music when Nat was growing up, and he could stand outside clubs and hear the likes of Jimmie Noone, Earl Hines, and of course Louis Armstrong. Nat's older brother, Eddie, was a gifted bass player, and they began to pick up work.

Incredibly enough, Nat wasn't singing in those early days, just playing piano. He got a job playing in the national tour of Eubie Blake's revue *Shuffle Along* when it came to Chicago. Nat was just sixteen when he was invited to join the company on the road. *Shuffle Along* is sometimes called the first all-black musical to reach white audiences, too. The show had been a huge hit on Broadway and in most of the rest of the country. But when the tour came to an end in Long Beach, California, Nat decided that he liked the sun and the laid-back style of California and that he would try his luck there. Success didn't come all at once, but he never had to look back.

Nat acquired the "King" in his name, he said, when a customer in a club he played put a paper hat on his head and said, "Look, King Cole." The customer sounds like a jerk. But the name stuck because of Nat's mastery of music and his dignified, regal bearing.

Southern California abounded with clubs and road joints in those days, and Nat formed a jazz quartet with Oscar Moore on guitar, Wesley Prince on string bass, and Nat at the piano. Nat said that one night the drummer didn't show up, and the Nat King Cole Trio was born.

To this day, I'm not sure I ever heard the real story of how it was that Nat began to sing in their act. You'd think a voice of his quality couldn't stay concealed for long. The story that Nat liked to tell (but he told his friends that it wasn't quite the whole story) was that one night a customer who'd had a little too much to drink (how many stories begin like that?) shouted from his seat that he wanted Nat, on the piano, to sing "Sweet Lorraine."

Nat told him, "We don't sing."

The club owner, according to the story, came over to whisper that the drunken customer was a big spender—and a big tipper. So Nat sang "Sweet Lorraine," the Cliff Burwell and Mitchell Parish song. It would become the Nat King Cole Trio's first hit in 1940.

I don't know what Nat left out of that story. But I always shared his artistic outlook that you shouldn't tamper with perfection.

Nat and I were both represented by the General Artists Corporation. We met unexpectedly in their offices in New York one afternoon in the mid-1950s. I had just enjoyed a few hits, including "Rags to Riches" and "Strangers in Paradise." But since Nat's own jazzy, brilliant "Straighten Up and Fly Right" had come out in 1943, Nat had joined the ranks of Frank Sinatra and Bing Crosby at the top of the charts. The signature round headquarters building of Capitol Records near Hollywood and Vine was called "The House that Nat Built," for all the records he had sold for Capitol.

We got on from the first, both personally and musically. We both loved jazz and found that our singing was influenced by the rhythms and syncopation of great jazz artists. I had taken the bus into New York that day from New Jersey, where I'd visited my mother in the home that I'd bought for her. Nat understood that. He'd gotten a home for his mother in Chicago.

Nat was booked to play the Chez Paree in Chicago in 1956, a great club in which he was always the returning hero. But President Dwight D. Eisenhower invited Nat to sing at the White House at the same time, and he had to bow out of his engagement at Chez Paree. He didn't want to leave his friends high and dry, so he called them up and said, "Get Tony Bennett."

I'll never forget what that meant to me. I'd had a couple of big hits but was still identified as a New York singer. Chicago was the most important market west of New York and had a busy, vibrant club scene. I'd never been able to crack that town with a major booking—but thanks to Nat "King" Cole, I was going into the best club, with his mark of approval. It was a wonderful vote of confidence that Nat "King" Cole's fans wouldn't be disappointed by this kid from Queens.

I wound up sharing the bill with the amazing Sophie Tucker. We were supposed to run for a few days, but as we left the stage that first night, Sophie turned to me and said, "Kid, we're going to run for a month." We did, and I knew that I had made it in Chicago.

(By the way: Sophie and I both had contracts stipulating that we'd have top billing. The owners of Chez Paree finessed this by putting her name on top on one side of the marquee and mine on the other—then made sure that Sophie, who was one of the biggest draws in show business at the time, was taken to the club only on the side of the street that had her name above mine.)

You'd think an artist booked for the White House at the special invitation of the president wouldn't be a victim of bigotry. But when Nat and his wife bought a huge, beautiful Tudor mansion in Hancock Park, a swanky district of Los Angeles, an attorney for one of their new neighbors said, "We don't want undesirable people coming here."

Nat replied with typical class—more class than the jerk deserved. "Neither do I," he said. That's why the name "King" fit him so well.

More alarmingly, one night in 1956, Nat was performing in Birmingham, Alabama, with Ted Heath, the great British bandleader, when three members of the Alabama Citizens' Council, a white supremacist group, rushed the stage. Reportedly, they wanted to kidnap Nat (they were appalled by a black man playing for a white audience but wouldn't mind taking money from the rich black man's family). The men were arrested before much of anything could happen. But Nat was knocked from his piano bench in the commotion, didn't finish the concert, and never—ever—played the South again.

Shortly after he appeared at the White House, NBC asked Nat to host his own weekly show on Monday nights. *The Nat "King" Cole Show* was the first major variety show to be hosted by a black entertainer and, boy, did he get great guests, including Ella Fitzgerald, Peggy Lee, Frankie Laine, Mel Tormé, and Eartha Kitt. When Nat "King" Cole invited you onto national television, you said yes.

But in the mid-1950s, NBC could never get a national sponsor for the show, and it ended—Nat himself suggested the cancellation—after just a year.

Nat told the newspapers, "I guess Madison Avenue is afraid of the dark."

It's a little funny to think these days that if an inebriated customer hadn't shouted, "Sing 'Sweet Lorraine'!" we might never have discovered Nat's supremely silky voice, which is still heard around the world, even in our dreams. Nat always said that he just sang the feelings that were in him. That sounds so simple, but of course it's not. He sang with the gifts of a great pianist: precision, shading, touch, and feeling. And I don't know of any other singer who had huge hits in at least three languages ("Darling, Je Vous Aime Beaucoup," including three albums in Spanish—though the Hotel Nacional de Cuba in Havana still wouldn't let him stay there when he recorded one of those albums in 1956; American-style segregation was the rule there, too).

When the rock revolution took over the charts, Nat managed better than some of the rest of us, with "Ramblin' Rose," "That Sunday, That Summer," and "Those Lazy-Hazy-Crazy Days of Summer" all hitting in the top ten.

Nat and I were both playing Las Vegas when "Ramblin' Rose" was the number one hit in America. I couldn't go to his shows, so I stopped by to visit during his rehearsal. He was working on a bit where he wanted to walk through the audience, singing. For some reason Jack Entratter, who owned the Sands, told Nat that he didn't like the idea (I wonder now if he worried that someone in the audience might misbehave). The room was dark, except for the light that followed Nat, so from the darkness, I just piped up, "Don't worry, Nat, you have the number one song in the country. Do whatever you want."

Both Nat and Jack cracked up, and Nat got his way.

Nat called me in the middle of 1964 to say that he was going to open a new hall in Los Angeles (he never quite mentioned that it was the Dorothy Chandler Pavilion) and that he wanted me, Ella Fitzgerald, and Count Basie to appear with him. Of course we all instantly agreed. Every few weeks, Nat would call just to check. "You've got it on your calendar, right?" he'd ask.

I didn't think much of anything when I didn't hear from Nat for a few weeks, but then I ran into Dean Martin.

"Nat has lung cancer," he told me.

Nat was in the hospital in Santa Monica, undergoing cobalt treatments, when the Dorothy Chandler Pavilion opened that December. Frank Sinatra took over the show, and it became a tribute to Nat. He was the talent that brought us all together, and his presence filled the hall on that historic first night.

Nat was briefly released from the hospital over the holidays but returned to the hospital in January and had a lung removed. You had to wonder what went through the mind of a great singer when he heard that the doctors had had to do that. But Nat was fighting for his life by then, not just a singing career. I know I would have stood in line to hear Nat "King" Cole sing with any breath that he could muster.

I started on tour with Bobby Hackett, the great cornet and trumpet player, early in 1965, and we were playing the Palmer House in Nat's own Chicago when we got word that Nat had died. He was just forty-five. I don't think most of the audience knew yet. Bobby and I looked at each other and asked, "What do we say? What do we play?" Then we simultaneously said, "'Sweet Lorraine.'"

I like to think that I would have eventually found a national audience for my music under any circumstances. But that night in his hometown, I knew how lucky I had been to receive Nat's endorsement and generosity. His faith in me, as much as anything else, gave me my own confidence.

And in 2001, when I got to sing "Stormy Weather" with Nat's beautiful and beloved daughter, Natalie, I felt as if I were somehow doing that last show with Nat that we never got the chance to do.

Then, a few years later, the beautiful Natalie Cole left us too soon, too.

New York Still Life

17

Rosemary Clooney

I never knew a greater natural singer than Rosemary Clooney. This big, beautiful blond girl from northern Kentucky
would stand up and sing as naturally as some gorgeous bird.

Mike Nichols, the great director, once said, "She sings like
Spencer Tracy acts." It was the highest compliment. But it also
sort of overlooked the hours Rosie had spent in rehearsals,
auditions, and smoky little clubs just over the Kentucky-Ohio
state line when she was a teenage act with her sister and they
worked every night, just hoping for a break.

Sometimes Rosie's great natural talent could cloak the troubles she wrestled with, even after—especially after—she was a
household name.

Rosie and I started out together at Columbia in the early
1950s. Frank Sinatra had left for Capitol Records, and Mitch
Miller was looking to come up with a new generation of singing
talent. I like to think he had a great eye for talent (I mean, he
signed me and Rosie, didn't he?).

But Mitch often had some peculiar ideas about what to do

with good singers. Mitch loved novelty songs that I guess he thought stood out from all the truly great popular music during that time.

Mitch was a great classical oboe and English horn player. I think he thought that, in a way, all popular songs were novelty items by comparison to the classical music he loved, even the most clever compositions by Cole Porter, Harold Arlen, and Yip Harburg.

During the same years that Rosie recorded great signature songs such as "Tenderly" and "Hey There," Mitch "convinced" her to sing "Come On-a My House" in 1951. It is almost certainly the worst song ever written by a great writer (William Saroyan). Bill and Ross Bagdasarian (who would later give the world the Chipmunks, a whole novelty act) wrote the song as a lark while driving across New Mexico. It was apparently based on Bill Saroyan's Armenian family.

I say "convinced" because although Mitch would argue with me about those kinds of songs and usually wind up sighing, swearing, and relenting, he threatened Rosie with contract cancellation, even after she'd made "Come On-a My House" the biggest single in America. She followed this with "Botch-a-Me" in 1952, and "Mambo Italiano" (which Bob Merrill, an otherwise great songwriter who would later write *Funny Girl*, wrote on a napkin and dictated to Mitch Miller from a pay phone in an Italian restaurant).

In her later years, Rosie told the *New York Times*, "I felt trapped and fabricated in the fifties, living up to other people's expectations." But she also admitted, "At the same time, you can't quarrel with success. If it hadn't been for 'Come on-a My House,' I probably wouldn't be here now."

Rosie became so well known for those novelty songs, she

said, that fans used to ask her to sing "How Much Is That Dog-gie in the Window," another Bob Merrill song that was actually a huge hit for Patti Page. But Rosie said, "They probably figure if it's a bad song, I must have done it."

Rosie knew hard times close up. Her father was a problem drinker, and her family broke up when she was fifteen. Her mother and younger brother, Nick, moved out to California (Nick would grow up to become a respected newsman, movie presenter, and social activist, and—notice I kept this for last—the father of a guy named George Clooney). Rosie and her sis-ter, Betty, stayed with their father. They began to sing outside the house, as much as anything to get out of the orbit of their father and their depressing home life.

WLW, just across the Kentucky River in Cincinnati, was one of America's great "clear channel" radio stations in the 1940s. When Rosie and Betty won the WLW talent contest in 1945, the broadcast beamed across the country. WLW created a show for the Clooney sisters and put them on the air seven nights a week (they earned $20 a night, Rosie once told me). Soon she was on her own, singing with big-name big bands and appearing on radio and television shows. Movies came calling.

Then, of course, the whole country fell in love with Rose-mary Clooney in 1954, when she sang "White Christmas" along with Bing Crosby, Danny Kaye, and Vera-Ellen in the final, tear-filled scene. Bing owned that song, of course. But go back to see and hear it: you'll hear Rosie's great, clear, warm voice carry above all the others.

Rosie's career went into overdrive after that. She was on all the television variety shows and toured with her old friend Bing Crosby. But in other ways, things were falling apart.

Rosie married José Ferrer twice. He was a great actor, and

that turned out to be the problem: he carried on a series of affairs with other women that he tried to conceal with his dramatic skills. Rosie loved and forgave him time and time again, but his infidelities wounded her.

She worked even harder to try to defeat her sadness. But then she began to take pills to help her work long hours, pills to help her sleep, pills to help her to wake up and start all over again. It was a prescription to put her into her own tailspin of depression and addiction.

"I loved downers," she once wrote in her memoir, "almost any kind. Loved the colors of them . . . I would just have a bouquet in my hands at night."

Rosie campaigned for Bobby Kennedy in 1968, when he ran for president. She was standing near him—close enough to touch him, close enough to feel that she should have saved him—when he was shot to death.

In many ways, Bobby's death threw Rosie over another edge. She somehow convinced herself that RFK wasn't really dead and it was all a cruel prank by the people who really ran the world. She would rant about it to everybody. But inside, I think she knew she was falling apart.

With bravery and daring, Rosie checked herself into the psychiatric ward of Mount Sinai Hospital in Los Angeles. Doctors helped her see that she might be suffering from bipolar disorder, in which she would swing from the highs of singing and the cheers of the audience who loved her to the lows of her loneliness in the middle of the night.

Rosie was in the hospital for a month. When she came out, it was hard for her to find work. People were a lot less knowledgeable and understanding about mental illness then, and Rosie had been admirably open about her challenges. She told me she had wound up singing in a lot of Holiday Inns. That's good, honest work for a performer, just not where you'd expect to see the star of *White Christmas* and one of the best-selling and greatest singers in America.

But Rosemary Clooney was always a good friend, and her friends came through as she always had for them. Bing did a special show to mark his 50th anniversary in show business and told her, "Rosie, I won't do it without you." She joined him, got rave reviews, and began to tour. She cooked up a music-and-comedy show with Rose Marie, Helen O'Connell, and Margaret Whiting, called *4 Girls 4*, that ran all over the country for eight years.

And she got back into the recording studio, this time on the Concord Jazz label, where she could finally sing the music that she loved and sang so beautifully. She recorded albums of music by George and Ira Gershwin (she lived in Ira Gershwin's old home in Beverly Hills, too), Irving Berlin, Johnny Mercer, Cole Porter, and many of the other greats.

A great collection, *Ballad Essentials*, has recently been rereleased. It will remind you of the power of Rosie's sincere feeling and beautifully lucid phrasing. Any male singer has to be careful when performing Arlen and Mercer's "One for My Baby (and One More for the Road)" to avoid comparisons with Frank Sinatra (those of us who dare to record that great song are always in the shadow of such comparisons). But listen to Rosie's version: she makes it truly her own. She pulls you along when she tells you that "But this torch that I found / Must be drowned / or it soon might explode."

Rosemary Clooney was back. She had brought herself back. She had worked hard to bring herself to the point where she could use her talent to express herself, not hide from her challenges, and to fill and enrich her life, as well as the lives of her fans, with the music she loved.

Her beloved sister and old singing partner, Betty, died of a brain aneurysm soon after Rosie's first new jazz recording. Rosie started a foundation in her sister's name, the Betty Clooney Foundation for Persons with Brain Injury, and produced a great 1977 autobiography, *This for Remembrance: The Autobiography of Rosemary Clooney, an Irish-American Singer*, written with Raymond Strait. It was made into a television movie starring Sondra Locke, a fine actress who could only lip-synch Rosie's songs. No one could sing as seemingly naturally and lyrically as Rosemary Clooney.

"I'll keep working as long as I live because singing has taken on the feeling of joy that I had when I started, when my only responsibility was to sing well," Rosie said.

I know that Rosie went through a lot. But she only wanted to share joys with people, including those of us who were her friends. When we got together, we laughed and joked about music, family, and show biz gossip. But she was always more interested in the stories of others. Singing was her life's work, and her way of lifting her life out of the ruts of sadness into which she sometimes fell.

Unfortunately, Rosie was a lifelong smoker (so many of us singers were in those days; famous singers even did cigarette commercials). She developed lung cancer in 2001 and was gone the next year. But she filled her seventy-four years with music, swings of highs and lows, recovery, joys, and ultimate triumph. She was a dear friend and a special talent who reminds me, even today, how much hard work, highs and lows, and simple human honesty it takes to sing as freely, naturally, and gorgeously as Rosemary Clooney.

Bangkok

Provence

18

Bill Evans

I've tried to live a life in which I've been proud of every song that I've ever recorded. But I'm prouder of nothing more than the two albums I did with the great pianist and composer Bill Evans, *The Tony Bennett/Bill Evans Album* in 1975 and *Together Again* in 1977.

Our friend Annie Ross, the great British jazz singer, proposed the idea one night when we were having dinner in London. Of course I knew the name. Bill Evans was probably the most legendary jazz pianist in the world at the time. He had played with Miles Davis's sextet when they recorded *Kind of Blue*, which is considered just about the most influential, and certainly the best-selling, jazz album of all time.

But I knew that Bill didn't often record with singers. His stellar use of impressionist harmonies and block chords (chords built directly below the melody, usually on the strong beats) were considered as innovative as those of Miles. But they would be an extra challenge for singers. Bill's genius usually had to be on its own. His solo 1963 album, *Conversations with Myself,* was one of the first uses of overdubbing, so that he could essentially accompany himself.

People spoke about him with awe and a little bit of mystery. Bill Evans was quiet and scholarly, a quintessential jazzman with classical training.

"Bill had this quiet fire that I loved on piano," Miles once said of him. "The sound he got was like crystal notes or water cascading down from some waterfall."

Bill happened to be playing in London at the time, so we went down to hear him. I was filled with awe, the way his hands seemed to hover over the keys, then lightly, precisely strike a note. I also found him to be friendly and approachable—a shy, warm kind of genius. He looked like a college professor, with round glasses softening his fierce, almost flinty eyes.

So in the spring of 1975, we worked out a deal to tape two albums with each other, one for Improv, which was then my label, and one for Bill's label, Fantasy.

"Keep your cronies at home, and I'll do the same," Bill told me. He wanted the sound of just two artists improvising with and inspiring each other without distraction. So it was just Bill, me, and an engineer in the studio, with Helen Keane, Bill's great manager, looking on through the glass as our producer.

It was one of the most intense musical experiences of my life. I'd suggest a tune, and Bill would say, "Good, let's try that." We'd find a key, then work it out note by note. No take—no measure—was the same as the next. Bill was always changing, jamming, winging it, and inviting me to come along.

You'd think you'd know a song—a standard like Henry Mancini and Johnny Mercer's "The Days of Wine and Roses"—but Bill would turn it over, note by note, phrase by phrase. It was like setting off on a great expedition and never knowing what was around the next turn—but you couldn't wait to find out.

I cherish those two albums we produced. Bill's own great song "Waltz for Debby," which was written for Bill's niece, Debby, and a song to break the heart of any father ("In her own sweet world / populated by dolls and clowns / and a prince and a big purple bear . . .") is on that first album, along with "The Days of Wine and Roses." The second includes Comden and Green's "Make Someone Happy" and Bill's own haunting "You Must Believe in Spring."

But Bill couldn't seem to find the spring for himself. At some point in the sixties or seventies, he had become hooked on cocaine, heroin, alcohol—to this day I'm not sure what and how much. We toured together after the albums and appeared

Houses in Trees

at Carnegie Hall, at the Smithsonian, and in a great television concert in the Netherlands. But Bill was so sick by then, he'd live just to go onstage for a set, then go off and lie down in his dressing room.

I loved Bill. A lot of people in show business (including me, I have to confess) used cocaine during that time, and we all kind of pretended with each other that it wasn't a problem. We told each other, in so many ways, that drugs were just what creative people used to open their imagination or soften the harsh realities of an unfair world.

But drugs began to take over Bill's life and leave room for little else. I had to ask him once, "What happened? Did someone hurt you?"

And Bill told me, "I wish they had. I wish somebody had broken my arm instead of sticking a needle in it for the first time. I wish somebody would have knocked me out so that I'd never touch it again."

The last time I talked to Bill was probably early 1980. He was able to track me down in a small town in Texas, where I was between gigs, and I didn't understand what was so urgent that he had to reach me so suddenly. I later learned that his beloved older brother, Harry, had taken his own life, which devastated Bill (he wrote one of his last songs for him, too, "We Will Meet Again," and it's beautiful, touching, and wrenching all at once).

"I wanted to tell you one thing," Bill said over the phone. "Just think truth and beauty. Forget about everything else. Just truth and beauty, that's all."

Bill had stopped his treatments for chronic hepatitis. It might have been a slow-motion way of joining his brother. Bill Evans left us in September 1980, and I can't stop thinking of all the music he left behind and all the music he didn't live to make.

His loss sobered me—in all ways. I missed my friend and creative partner. And, I knew, I'd be foolhardy not to see Bill's loss as an alarm bell for my own life.

Those two great albums we recorded? You practically couldn't give them away when they came out. But now they're considered classics and have sold far more in reissue. Sometimes the world just needs to catch up with what you're doing. As Bill Evans said, truth and beauty, that's all.

Spring in Manhattan

19

Jackie Kennedy

Rosemary Clooney and I played Loew's Capitol Theatre in Washington, DC, in 1951. The *Washington Times-Herald* sent a young photojournalist to snap our photo and interview us. She was smart and pretty, and we enjoyed talking to her.

A few years later, I got a call from Rosie.

"Tony, Tony," she said. "Remember the gal who interviewed us in Washington? It's Jackie. *Jackie Kennedy.* Jacqueline *Bouvier* Kennedy. Remember?"

And then I did.

I think of that story now and then, not just because, like most Americans, I loved and admired Jackie Kennedy. I think of that meeting, and it reminds me of the wisdom of one of the oldest truisms in show business: be nice to everyone; you never know when you'll meet them again.

The stagehand, busboy, or mailroom clerk you meet on

the way up may one day become the producer, owner, or agent you need to ask for a job. The young photographer who comes to your dressing room, snaps a few shots, and shyly asks a few questions may one day become first lady of the United States—or president.

Central Park

Louvre, Paris

Pablo Picasso

P ablo Picasso worked for decades to be able to draw like a child. I certainly don't compare my own painting to the great master of twentieth-century art. But any kind of artist can be inspired by Picasso's ceaseless, restless innovation. The greatest visual artist of his time was never satisfied with his achievements. He never stopped—not even into his nineties—experimenting, tinkering, inventing, and opening new frontiers.

You don't have to be ninety (like me) to find that inspiring.

I've walked around some of the great art museums in the world to see his work and, in a way, drink from it. Picasso's father, José Ruiz, was an artist and a teacher, and young Pablo apparently had an art pencil or a paintbrush in his hand from an early age. He became so quickly accomplished at drawing and painting that his father more or less gave up his own painting.

Picasso was just fifteen—fifteen!—when he painted his first major work, *First Communion*. It shows his sister Lola making her First Communion. The folds in her white dress almost rustle. The candles on the altar seem to flicker. The painting is as finely, minutely detailed as any that you see by Rembrandt or El Greco.

But by the early twentieth century, Picasso had entered what's now called his Blue Period. There's a picture I've seen at New York's Solomon R. Guggenheim Museum called *Woman Ironing* that Picasso finished in 1904. It shows a woman, bent over and haggard, pushing a hot, heavy iron across a shapeless white expanse. The entire painting is tinged with a blue light with streaks of gray, and just a couple of light flashes of flesh tones in the woman's arms. Picasso has dramatically reduced the details in the portrait, so that your eyes are drawn to just a few strands of hair that seem to hang from her head in exhaustion and the large gray shrouds of her eyes. At the time, he was down-and-out in Paris. That period was indeed blue in all ways.

But just a few years later, he entered his Rose Period. He painted lots of circus performers, and for the first time in years added bold strokes of orange, pink, and red. Then he was on to his Cubist Period, in which he reimagined the basic shape of objects and people. His 1910 *Girl with a Mandolin*, which is at New York's Museum of Modern Art, is all beige and gray, depicting a girl with light brown hair, holding a mandolin in a series of bare, spare planes and half spheres (the painting was a bequest to the museum by the late Nelson Rockefeller, who had extraordinary taste in modern art).

By the 1920s, Picasso was on to what would become known as surrealism. His 1919 *Sleeping Peasants*, a watercolor and pencil composition that's also at the Museum of Modern Art, shows a man and a woman on a bale of hay who are folded into each other (her blouse is open, and their feet are bare; a lot of critics say it must be after a real roll in the hay). Each human feature—toes, knuckles, legs, throats—seems swollen. But the colors are bright, vivid, and varied.

Of course Picasso's most famous painting, *Guernica*, hung for years at MoMA before the museum decided to return it to Spain. For that historic painting, the master went back to black, grays, and smoky whites to show a mother grieving over a dead child in her arms, a horse buckling in pain, a remnant of a human arm still holding on to a broken sword. It epitomizes my view of war perfectly.

Picasso painted it after the pitiless destruction of the Basque town of Guernica by German and Italian warplanes in 1937, during the Spanish Civil War. But you don't see any national or political symbols in the painting, just shattered women, children, and animals. It's kept that great painting timeless, as eloquent about Syria as it was about Spain.

Picasso was staggeringly prolific. It's estimated that he produced about fifty thousand works of art in his ninety-one years, from drawings to prints to paintings to sculptures. And he never stopped drawing, painting, and creating. But what you see, as he grew more experienced and wise but no less bold, is how, year by year, he cast off technique and tricks to draw and paint clear, simple, elegant lines that conveyed a world of feeling with no distracting superfluity. In a way, that's what children do: put all they feel into a stroke or line; except with Picasso, it's as if he tried to pack decades of what he had learned into just that slender line.

I hope I've learned more about that in my own painting. And I've learned to try to apply that idea to my music. To sing with a simple, clear, elegant line that invites the audience to open their hearts and minds.

San Francisco

Sadie Vimmerstedt

Y ou don't have to pretend that you know the name Sadie Vimmerstedt, much less pronounce it. Sadie was
a mother and grandmother who worked in a cosmet-
ics store in Youngstown, Ohio, and loved music, especially the
songs of Johnny Mercer.

Around 1957, the story of Frank Sinatra leaving his first
wife, Nancy, for Ava Gardner, then Ava dropping Frank for a
bullfighter, was splashed across front pages around the world.
That public drama inspired Sadie Vimmerstedt to pick up a
pen and write two lines: "I want to be around to pick up the
pieces / When somebody breaks your heart."

She put the two lines in an envelope that she addressed to:
"Johnny Mercer, Songwriter, Los Angeles, California." The US
Postal Service, no doubt through rain, sleet, and dark of night,
routed it to the American Society of Composers, Authors and
Publishers, which deals in music rights. They routinely routed
it to Johnny.

Fishermen, San Francisco

Johnny read the lines. He liked them so much, in fact, that he wrote the song, both the music and the lyrics. He asked me to record it, and in 1963, "I Wanna Be Around" became one of my biggest hits ever.

Johnny Mercer gave Sadie Vimmerstedt a big slice of the royalties—so much that she could leave Youngstown and spend the rest of her life traveling to the places she'd only heard about in songs, like Paris and Rome. I'd get postcards from Sadie from all over the world.

By the way: Frank recorded a cover version the next year. I don't know if he realized that, in a way, he had already contributed to the song.

People often ask me, "Where are the new Tony Bennetts?" But I wonder, when it comes to people who know and love quality popular songs, "Where are the new Sadie Vimmerstedts?"

Paris

Lena Horne

I worked with Lena Horne at what I would guess to be just about the lowest point in her life. We got together in 1972 to tape a one-hour television special, produced by Lord Lew Grade, at the Palladium in London. In the previous year and a half, Lena had lost her father, Edwin, her son, Teddy, who was just thirty when he died of a kidney disease, and her husband, the great music director Lennie Hayton (they were separated but still close).

Lena's heart must have been aching. But she was the picture of professionalism: always on time, rehearsed, and ready. She showed me not just how to carry on but how your work can help you find a peaceful center when the world around you seems to be falling apart.

It is hard to explain Lena Horne's career to people these days. She was undoubtedly one of the most beautiful women of the age, with dazzling dark eyes, bright skin, almost like burnished gold, and a roguish smile. But she was born in an America that was still segregated, and all of her beauty, popularity, and talent could not overcome the racism that still flourished.

Lena told me that once, when she had entertained US troops at home during World War II, she saw that white German prisoners of war were seated in front of black American soldiers. She had gotten down off the stage, walked to the first row in which black soldiers were seated, and opened her act. You couldn't rattle Lena Horne. But you wouldn't blame her for seething below.

Lena was singing at Harlem's famous Cotton Club by the time she was a teenager. She found club life hard and moved to Hollywood, where she became almost the first black star to sign a contract with a major studio, MGM. She starred in 1942's *Panama Hattie*, 1943's *Stormy Weather* (flip a three-sided coin to decide which is the definitive version of the song—Ethel Waters's, Judy Garland's, or Lena's), and 1943's Vincente Minnelli's *Cabin in the Sky* (in which a famous scene of Lena singing in a bubble bath—and just a bubble bath—was cut by censors).

What prevented the most glamorous, gifted, and beautiful singing star of her time from becoming the leading American film star? Race, pure and simple.

Lena Horne could almost never be cast in a leading role, because scenes featuring black actors were often snipped out so that a major studio film could be shown in the South. That's why scenes with great entertainers such as Louis Armstrong, Cab Calloway, Eddie Anderson, and Lena were often musical numbers that were incidental to the plot. They would show the whole film in New York or Chicago, then the censored—let's be blunt about this—segregated version in Atlanta, Birmingham, or, for that matter, the nation's capital, Washington, DC.

Lena really wanted to play the role of Julie in MGM's 1951

redo of the Jerome Kern–Oscar Hammerstein musical *Show Boat*. Can you imagine Lena Horne singing "Can't Help Lovin' Dat Man"? (In fact, you don't have to imagine it: Lena had already sung the song in a 1946 film, *Till the Clouds Roll By*, a biopic, as we'd call it today, about Jerome Kern.)

But when the time came to make *Show Boat*, MGM refused to cast their most glamorous black star as Julie LaVerne, the actress who is thrown out of her theater company for being half black. Ava Gardner, a white star and Lena's good friend, got the part. That must have hurt.

Lena got sick and tired of Hollywood, I think. She also lost some jobs because of Hollywood blacklisting. Lena was a big supporter of civil rights before the activism of the 1950s and '60s, and she was friends with Paul Robeson. The kinds of people who enforced the blacklist considered civil rights to be part of a Communist conspiracy.

So she went back on the road, into nightclubs and concerts, and became just about the biggest draw in the United States. Her 1957 record *Lena Horne at the Waldorf Astoria* became the biggest-selling record by a woman in the history of RCA. She was also nominated for a Tony Award for Best Actress in a Musical for her role in *Calypso*. She became a staple on variety shows in the United States, and then we got together in London.

Lena brought a degree of intensity, even to rehearsals, that I had never seen. She didn't see rehearsals as a chance to make mistakes so much as a way of learning how to do things right from the start. We opened our show together with the Burt Bacharach–Hal David song "The Look of Love" and George Harrison's "Something." Then Lena did a set on her own, I did a set, and we ended with a medley of Harold Arlen songs.

What a show it was, night after night. Lena felt her recent losses, but she almost never talked about her sadness or setbacks. Out of principle and character, Lena Horne was a complete, pure, and superlative professional when she came to the stage. We went on to tour the United Kingdom and United States for a couple of years and then brought the show back to London for a farewell.

Lena tried to retire a few times. But people kept calling her back to make special appearances onstage and on television (including, memorably, on *The Muppet Show*—where she sang one of my favorite versions of Joe Raposo's "Sing!"). Finally in 1981, the Nederlander family decided that if she wasn't going to retire, they wanted Lena to open the 41st Street theater on which they had put their name. That show, *Lena Horne: The Lady and Her Music*, ran for years on Broadway and on tour around the world and won a special Tony for Lena. It's still the longest-running one-person show in Broadway history.

I feel privileged to have performed with Lena Horne, and I try to take strength from the resilience she displayed in the face of setbacks and heartbreak. I think of it as a kind of code of conduct for great performers: when life sends you difficulties or misfortunes, don't get mad or sad—get busy. That's what Lena Horne did.

Monet Garden #4

Monet Garden #6

Maurice Chevalier

A lot of Americans thought of Maurice Chevalier as the quintessential Frenchman. But I was lucky enough to see him perform when I was a kid, and he became my idea of the quintessential entertainer.

My uncle Dick Suraci, my mother's younger brother, had a job at the ticket office of the Broadway Theatre. Uncle Dick had been a hoofer in vaudeville, dancing under the name Dick Gordon. But as his knees grew older and the vaudeville circuit dried up, Uncle Dick got the job at the box office. But he didn't seem disheartened by working offstage, away from the footlights.

"Every day," he said, "I get to go to work at the theater."

I knew I was interested in show business. I sang at family dinners from the time I was six or so and enjoyed the attention. Uncle Dick, I think, wanted to encourage me, but he also wanted me to learn that show business was a real business, not a hobby; it would take hard work, dedication, and discipline.

So Uncle Dick took me into the city one day because he wanted me to see Maurice Chevalier rehearse and perform. Maurice's extraordinary boulevardier charm didn't betray some of the tough times he'd had.

He was singing and dancing in Paris nightclubs as a teenager. Then he was drafted in the buildup to World War I. With scant training, he was sent into the frontline trenches with thousands of other scared young French kids. He quickly got wounded in the first weeks of the war by hot shrapnel in the back that punctured a lung. He was captured by the Germans.

He spent two years in a German prisoner of war camp, which couldn't have been like the Ritz. But he wound up meeting a lot of British POWs, who taught him English. Even then, he wanted to play London and New York.

After the war, Maurice became a headliner at the Casino de Paris, during a time when it thronged with US and British soldiers on their way home. He learned their jokes, their slang, and their songs and began to work ragtime, jazz, and the blues into his act. Finally he was booked into London and then went off to tour the United States.

When talkies came in, Maurice went out to Hollywood and quickly became what amounted to America's image of a suave, singing Frenchman in movie after movie, including *Innocents of Paris* and *The Big Pond* (an interesting 1930 film with dialogue by Preston Sturges, simultaneously shot in English and French versions, with Maurice and Claudette Colbert, who had been raised speaking French in her family).

I sat quietly in a middle row in the darkened Broadway Theatre to watch Maurice rehearse. I saw that a lot of work went into being so suave and effortless, which I'm pretty sure is exactly what Uncle Dick wanted me to see. Maurice said later that having what he considered an average singing voice "made me look for something to make me different from a hundred other crooners who are neither good nor bad."

When Maurice hit the stage for that matinee, I noticed the mutual respect between him and the musicians. They'd just met and had grown up in different places. But they'd shared a day of hard work in a creative enterprise and understood each other in a special way. Maurice made a point, too, of introducing each musician by name to the audience. It was a mark of respect, a way of letting the audience know that he appreciated the professionals who helped make him look good.

I didn't meet Maurice that day. But I got to tell him the story years later when we met as performers, and he smiled and said, "Tony, it's important for the audience to know about all the artists who are onstage."

So from the time I started singing onstage, I've made it a point to know and introduce the musicians to the audience, too. Those talented individuals are essential to the music we make and love. I think the audience welcomes the chance to give them their appreciation, too.

Years later, Maurice was performing at the Waldorf-Astoria when the New York musicians' union went on strike. That was at a time when many club owners were eager to replace live bands with recorded music and save money. Maurice didn't want to undercut the musicians with whom he had worked so closely by singing along to a tape. But he also knew that people had bought tickets weeks and months in advance to see his show. Many of them wanted to see him to celebrate an anniversary, a birthday, or an engagement. He didn't want to disappoint them.

So he went on as scheduled that night—and sang a cappella. It was utter showmanship, and he earned a standing ovation after practically each number.

To this day, I try to sing one song a cappella, just my lone, bare voice, unamplified, in a club or theater. Maurice showed me how powerful that can be. It reminds an audience: This isn't a recording. We're here together for a once-in-a-lifetime experience.

Academy of Art, Venice

Central Park, West Side

24

Frank Sinatra

Frank Sinatra did one of the most caring things that any colleague of mine in the industry has done in my entire career, and I will always be grateful to him for that alone. In the autumn of 1974, Frank knew that my mother was nearing the end of her life, and was pretty sure that she and I would be watching his televised concert from Madison Square Garden, *Sinatra: The Main Event.* At one point between songs, talking his way into Vernon Duke's "Autumn in New York," Frank ad-libbed, "Tony Bennett is my favorite guy in the whole world." My mother's face lit up like Times Square. I'd call it a small, loving gesture, except that, of course, it was seen and heard by millions of people. I will never forget how much Frank's gesture meant to my mom and to me.

Frank Sinatra has been an important part of my life since I was nine, when our family would listen to *Major Bowes' Original Amateur Hour.* I was an original bobby-soxer. I'd go to his shows at the Paramount, with thousands of other teenagers, and stay for all seven shows, with girls all around me faint-ing for Frank. (There would later be academic papers written about this phenomenon, which seemed to escalate because we couldn't bring food to our seats or go out to use the bathroom without giving up our places—so kids would faint.)

What I remember most vividly about Frank from those years when I saw him from a distance, when I was just a fan who was not yet his friend, was the utter clarity of his phrasing. He worked at it as hard as Meryl Streep ever would to perfect an ac-cent. Frank sang every vowel and consonant of every word; it's one of the (many) reasons why all the great songwriters wanted to work with him.

Listen to Frank's speaking voice in one of his concerts or on the old radio shows, or in one of his great movies, like *From Here to Eternity* or *A Hole in the Head*. He sounds like—he is—a Jersey guy. Then listen to "Fly Me to the Moon," "The Lady is a Tramp," or his truly astounding rendition of "Ol' Man River," in which Frank does not slip into dialect but enunciates every phrase. That clarity was part of revealing the heart of a song, and Frank's own heart. In his early days, Frank was part of a singing group called the Hoboken Four, who won the contest one week in September 1935, when our family was listening. When Major Edward Bowes asked, in his booming, intimidat-ing voice, "Who will speak for this group?" I heard a confident young voice come right back at him: "I will. I'm Frankie. We're looking for jobs. How 'bout it?" Frank Sinatra was all of nine-teen.

The jobs kept coming, too. Frank and the group became such popular winners that Major Bowes decided to keep bring-ing them back, but under different names. One week they'd be the Seacaucus Cockamamies. Another they'd be the Bayonne

Baccalàs (baccalà is an Italian delicacy of dried salt cod). But whatever they were called, Frank's group always won.

By 1939, Frank was singing with the Harry James Orchestra. Within a year, the great Tommy Dorsey recruited him for his band. Frank and Tommy would become famous together, argue together, have a nasty split, and wind up being friends again. When I look back on it, I think their split was inevitable: no band, even the Tommy Dorsey Orchestra, would be big enough to keep Frank Sinatra to itself. But in time, each of them grew to see what they owed the other. By 1940, Frank's singing and popularity put Tommy's band ahead of all others. Frank always told me that Tommy taught him how to be a better singer, a better artist, and a better man.

Frank studied the way Tommy played the jazz trombone and applied those lessons to his own voice. He worked to expand his breathing (he spent a lot of time swimming underwater at public pools, among other exercises) so that he could sing two or three lines without taking a breath. It made the audience pay attention to and hang on his every phrase. It made, to quote Tommy, the "skinny kid with big ears" into an object of adoration. The "swooning" that began for Frank was for the way he would sweep you away with that clear, lyrical, soaring, sweet voice.

I didn't get to meet Frank until the spring of 1956, when I was given the chance to take over Perry Como's slot on a summer replacement show. I was just coming off the success of my recording of "Stranger in Paradise," which made a hit of a song from *Kismet*, the Robert Wright and George Forrest musical that had the bad luck of premiering in the middle of a New York newspaper strike.

I soon discovered that though I was taking over Perry's slot that summer, I was hardly taking over his show. *The Perry Como Show* was a full-scale production, week after week, with big-name guest stars, elaborate sets, and a full orchestra and chorus. But NBC decided to save money during the summer (when, to be fair, the audiences were smaller) by making the "Tony Bennett Keeps Perry Como's Slot Warm during the Summer" show a bargain-basement production, with just me on an empty stage with a ten-piece orchestra. I worried if anyone would watch, at least for more than ten minutes. Frank had repaired relations with Tommy Dorsey by then, and was playing the Paramount again with Tommy and his orchestra. I decided to ask Frank for advice.

I had heard in show business circles that Frank liked my singing. But even now, whatever possessed me to show up, unannounced, backstage to ask for the favor of his advice still baffles me a little. Some people who had been on the periphery of Frank's entourage told me that it wouldn't be a good idea to approach him. They said he could be moody and unpredictable. But I went to the backstage entrance of the Paramount, where they knew me pretty well from my own shows, and someone slipped back to tell him that Tony Bennett would like to see him. I waited just a few nervous minutes before a man led me back to Frank's dressing room. I took a breath. Frank was unperturbed by the interruption. I told him about my worries for the summer replacement show, and Frank listened with great courtesy. Then the biggest man in show business said, "Tony, it's only natural that you should be nervous. And it's good. It means that you care. If you don't care about what you're doing, why should the audience? But when the audience sees how much you want to please them, they'll root for you. Remember, they're only there because they already want to like you. Let them know how much that means to you, and they'll love you. They'll support you. Work hard for them, and they'll cheer hard for you."

Our meeting lasted only a few minutes—but I walked back out onto Broadway feeling as if my feet weren't touching the ground. I knew Frank was right. And he made me feel as if I could rise above my fears and do anything. Artists do that for all of us. On that day, Frank taught me to trust and use my anxieties to sharpen and key up my performance. Once you get started, the butterflies in your stomach can help you soar. From that day on, Frank and I were friends.

Now and then, someone who knew him would pass along a compliment. I worked with a great drummer named Mickey Scrima at a gig in Dallas, who said to me once, "Do you know what Frank says about you?" Mickey said, "Frank said about you, 'That kid's got four sets of balls.'" Frank Sinatra changed my life in another immediate and direct way: he got me gigs. A lot of people at the top of the heap wouldn't go out of their way to help someone else try to climb up there.

When Duke Ellington and I performed at the Americana Hotel in Miami Beach in 1960, Frank knew that there was a convention of hotel owners meeting nearby. He brought them in to see our show, and they seemed to have a great time.

For the next ten years, I got bookings in classy spots, and they traced back to that one night.

Then, a few years later, he changed my life again. He was the cover story of *Life* magazine on April 23, 1965. In talking about the music and singers he enjoyed, Frank said, "For my money, Tony Bennett is the best singer in the business. He excites me when I watch him. He moves me. He's the singer who gets across what the composer has in mind, and probably a little more."

Before the ink on the magazine was dry, the phone began to ring off the hook. I was on the road. My manager called and read me the quote. I had to get hold of my emotions. Being called "the best singer in the business" by Frank Sinatra was like . . . well, no simile is really necessary, is it? But I hope it didn't go to my head. I don't think it did. On the contrary: it gave me a lot to live up to. It's still in my mind every time I take the stage.

Frank became just about my best friend. But I wasn't a member of the Rat Pack or his personal entourage. We had dinner and drinks, and we had laughs. I'd fly in for Frank's birthday party every year—legendary, historic parties, with Nelson Riddle in one corner, Count Basie in another, Marilyn Monroe, Cary Grant, Fred Astaire, Kim Novak, Dean, Sammy—I could go on. There'd be great music, fabulous food, and gorgeous people all over his place. I used to wonder why, year after year, Frank would make sure I was seated next to a famous old entertainment lawyer and not Cary, Fred, or even Tommy Lasorda, the Dodgers' manager, who was Frank's dear friend.

One year I finally figured it out: the lawyer was one of the most influential men in Hollywood. Once again, Frank was trying to do me a favor.

Of course I've heard some of the stories about other sides of his personality. I just never saw them. The Frank Sinatra I knew was always a gentleman, a devoted friend, and a man of legendary generosity. He'd call producers and club owners to get work for people who needed it, and he'd get the best doctors in the country to make time to see a parking attendant if he required medical help. He helped his closest friends in a hundred different ways, as well as scores of people he'd just heard about. He'd see someone on the news who had been burned out of her home or a guy who had lost a factory job after twenty or thirty years and send that person a check—no publicity, no attention. It was just something that he did to try to even up the odds in life.

I once read *The Autobiography of Benvenuto Cellini*, the memoir of a sculptor in Renaissance Italy whose works were coveted by popes and monarchs. Cellini had a keen sense of justice and injustice. He would draw his sword when he thought someone was being unfair, whatever his rank or wealth. I sent Frank a copy of the book and wrote inside it, "If Shirley MacLaine's philosophy is right, you must have been this cat in another life." I wonder what life Frank is on to now.

One night in the early '70s, Ralph Sharon and I were playing Caesars Palace in Las Vegas when Frank asked his pal Vido Musso, the saxophonist, to set up dinner after our respective shows. It was a small restaurant way off the Strip where Frank could unwind and talk about the journey of his life, from Hoboken to the seven shows a day at the Paramount, to Ava and Columbia, and then down in the dumps, to the Oscars, and then back up the mountain to the top. There was a piano in the joint. We started late and stayed late, and just before the first sunlight began to streak into the desert sky through the windows, Frank said, "Tony, before we leave, it would mean a lot to me if you and Ralph could do a song."

What else could we say but yes? It meant a lot to us, too. Ralph and I conferred and quickly settled on a Jerome Kern tune, with lyrics by Otto Harbach:

Olden days, golden days
days of mad romance and love . . .

Sad am I, glad am I
For today I'm dreamin' of yesterdays.

By the time we left, the sun was spreading an orange glow over the ride home, and Ralph and I felt we'd been blessed to have an extraordinary moment.

Frank and I shared a stage just a few times together over the years. It was always a special occasion. One time that means just about the most to me was a night we both performed at Bally's in Atlantic City in 1988.

I wore a white tux—Frank wore a black one. We went back and forth between our various hits and joined in together on "The Lady Is a Tramp." Toward the end of the show, Frank said, "Here's one of the prettiest songs in the American

Los Angeles Still Life

library, and no one sings it prettier than this guy." It was a generous setup for me to sing "I Left My Heart in San Francisco." Then I handed the orchestra off to Frank for him to sing his fabulous John Kander and Fred Ebb anthem "New York, New York," singing it in a fervent way that makes the song a hymn for everyone, from Ketchikan to Key West, who struggles to do his best and strives to reach the top. Then Frank invited this son of Astoria, Queens, to join him to repeat the last few lines:

> *If I can make it there*
> *I'm gonna make it anywhere*
> *It's up to you, New York, New York!*

We took our bows, the houselights dimmed, and people threw bouquets onto the stage. Frank reached out for an armful of roses, removed a flower, and put it into my lapel. We walked offstage to a standing ovation, arm in arm.

He was my best friend.

Christos Gates, Central Park

25

Jimmy Durante

I was a lucky high school kid when I saw the greatest enter-tainer in America. He sure didn't look the part. He was hunched over, bald, and—he'd be the first to say this—wouldn't be confused with Errol Flynn. He played the piano with more zest than finesse. And he sang—barely—in a croaky, raspy voice.

But boy, did Jimmy Durante have personality.

I was probably about fourteen or fifteen and a student at In-dustrial Arts High School when a girl who must have liked me a little more than I liked her (because I'm afraid I just can't re-member her name) invited me to go to the Copacabana. I think her father had some connection to the club—good enough to get us in and a pretty good table.

Jimmy Durante was the star. He owned the stage from the moment he sauntered out in his squashed fedora and tux, plopped down at the piano, and began to play, almost as if he were banging out a melody on a bunch of cans. He sang almost like a man who was drowning and shouting for help. And every minute or so, he would lift his hands and say, "Stop da music! Stop da music!" to tell some joke. He was outrageous, original, and totally marvelous.

The girl took me backstage, and as we approached Jimmy's dressing room, we saw just his nose—the famous Durante *schnozzola*, as he called it—poke out from one side of the door frame. Then the rest of Jimmy turned the corner, laughing, to say hello.

He invited us in. He put his hand, in a fatherly way, on my head. I wish I could better remember what we talked about, but I remember that he both entertained us and really listened to a couple of kids. Jimmy himself had left school in the seventh grade to enter show business. He had formed an act with his cousin, who was also named Jimmy Durante, then branched out on his own, playing ragtime and jazz and adding his signature humor. "I got a million of 'em!"

He went out to Hollywood and became a big star on the strength of his charm, ingenuity, and humor. Hollywood had thousands of handsome men and pretty good singers. But there was only one Jimmy Durante. He made a lot of films that are hard to remember now—*Blondie of the Follies*, *The Phantom President*, *What! No Beer?* (Buster Keaton's last film), and *Palooka*.

Jimmy usually played the comic sidekick who had a featured musical number. He sang his own song, "Inka Dinka Doo," to a store window mannequin in *Palooka*, and the record of the song he recorded thereafter became one of the biggest hits of the 1930s. A few other singers have dared to record it, including Sammy Davis, Jr., and Ann-Margret. But really, only Jimmy's version is remembered today. You needed his charm

Portugal

and personality to put across a song that is not much more than those three made-up words.

Jimmy was a complete entertainer. He was not a great singer, dancer, or piano player, but he put warmth, sincerity, and humor into all he did. That made him a singular talent.

I say—as Jimmy would say himself—that he wasn't a "great" singer. But what he had was a great soul. There is no greater version of "Make Someone Happy," that wonderful Jule Styne and Comden and Green song, than Jimmy's. When he gasps as much as sings, "One you've found her / Build your world around her," you feel shivers. Jimmy makes it the cry of a man who has really learned about the value of love.

Some of that was an act, of course. But it was also not an act at all. Jimmy Durante was a kind, funny, and truly loving man. His dedication to causes for children was legendary. He helped build the Fraternal Order of Eagles' programs for handicapped and abused children (now called the Jimmy Durante Children's Fund). He raised tens of millions of dollars for the fund, and when the fraternal order asked him, "What can we do for you?" Jimmy told them, "Help da kids." He had never been abused or handicapped as a child. But he had vivid memories of being teased about his appearance.

"I was hurt so deep," he told a biographer, Gene Fowler, "that I made up my mind never to hurt anybody else, no matter what. I never made jokes about anybody's big ears, their stuttering, or about them being off their nut."

Jimmy had a great gift of expression, in all ways. In the 1950s, when the plays of Tennessee Williams, William Inge, and Eugene O'Neill were big on Broadway (briefly), Jimmy lamented the disappearance of the musical by saying, "Everything went psychological!"

And of course, he signed off all of his shows by saying, "Good night, Mrs. Calabash, wherever you are." We learned later that it was a salute to his first wife, Jeanne Olsen, who had died unexpectedly in 1943; Calabash was his way of saying Calabasa, a small town in the Santa Monica Mountains that they had visited and loved (though residents of Calabash, North Carolina, are still convinced it was their town).

I got to perform on the same bill as Jimmy a few times and would call him my friend. But I never took the opportunity to tell him what his pat on the head had meant to me when I was a high school student.

Seeing Jimmy Durante's act and the joy he always gave people showed me how the show business life could be rewarding, enriching, and valuable, however demanding and competitive. The memory of Jimmy Durante reminds me today not to hesitate to tell people what they mean to me or figure that I'll have plenty of time to say what I want to. He taught me to tell people what you want to right now, while it's on your mind. While you know they are here to appreciate it.

New York Snowstorm

26

Astoria, Queens, New York

I figure it's a blessing for anyone to be born in New York. Where else can you see so much of the world in a single city block? But I feel especially blessed that my family wound up in Queens.

Both my father's family, the Benedettos, and my mother's family, the Suracis, were from Calabria, at the toe of the Italian peninsula. It's a beautiful region, ringed by mountains, forests, and the sea. They began to leave at different times in the late 1890s because of a crop blight that impoverished millions of people all over Italy. And, to be sure, they left because they'd heard about the promise of America.

It is hard for us to appreciate the courage of our families when they came over to America (and every American family, save for Native Americans, has "come over" at some point). To be from a small town where everyone knows everyone, then leave everything you know and cross an ocean, and then to arrive and try to make new lives in a place where you don't even speak the language, with people from all over the world brushing up against one another—that's truly courage. That's why my heart is with immigrants we see all over the world today.

My mother's parents, Antonio and Vincenza Suraci, were the first to make that trip to America. They left Italy in 1899 with their two children, my aunt Mary and my uncle Frank. My mother was along, too: Grandma Vincenza was a month pregnant with her.

After a rough journey that took three weeks in the sweltering hold of a steamship, they sailed into New York Harbor and finally took their first steps on Ellis Island. They filled out forms in English that they couldn't understand and tried to reply to questions they found puzzling. They were given brusque physical exams, almost like farm animals, knowing all the while that even a slight physical ailment, or an answer to a question that an inspector didn't understand or like, could get them sent back across the ocean.

But Antonio and Vincenza passed whatever tests there were and settled among other families they'd known in Calabria and families from other regions of Italy, in lower Manhattan, on Mulberry Street. Hundreds of thousands of families would wind up there.

Around the time the first Suracis arrived, my other grandmother, Maria Benedetto, was widowed. This is rough anywhere, but especially in a small town in Italy. Maria decided to join her sister Vincenza in New York. The Benedettos came over to America in a few waves, my father finally arriving in 1906.

The neighborhood known as Little Italy was closely packed with old, musty five-story brownstone tenement buildings where people lived in teeming apartments that overlooked dingy alleys. Sunlight was scarce. Kids often slept four and six to a room, sharing beds and sprawled on sofas. Three or four families often shared kitchens and bathrooms. During the day, there would be scores of pushcart vendors on the crowded, noisy sidewalks, shouting out the fruit and vegetables for sale above the rumble of streetcars and the din and dust of horses and a few gas-belching automobiles. Every hour seemed like rush hour, with swarms of people trying to push and pull packed carts down busy streets.

All of my grandparents were happy to be in America. But Little Italy was dirt, smoke, noise, and trash, not like the green fields of Calabria. There were life, color, and closeness in those neighborhoods. Maybe that's why so many moviemakers love the period. But everyday life was also demanding.

My mother's father, Antonio Suraci, also became the first to leave Little Italy, although not by more than a few blocks. He moved the family over to 12th Street between 1st and 2nd Avenues to start a wholesale business that sold fruits and vegetables to the pushcart owners. He'd get to work before the sun rose, so the vendors could be out at first light, and he didn't leave his small warehouse for home until it was dark.

My grandfather was good at business but felt uncomfortable working in English and with numbers. Every day, he would give the money he made to my grandmother. My grandmother would pay out what they had to (in time, they would have seven children) and put whatever was left over inside a trunk under their bed. Then they'd both start all over again the next day.

My father's sister, Antoinette, moved even a little farther. She and her husband, Demetri, opened a grocery store on 6th Avenue at 52nd Street in 1918, in what were then the "wilds" of midtown Manhattan. Half a century later, that location became the spot where CBS would build its sleek corporate headquarters, designed by Eero Saarinen in 1965. A CBS division president once told me that the sale of my records built at least ten floors of that building. Even if that was a flattering exaggeration, I like to think there's the story of America in there: the nephew of the folks who owned a small grocery on that spot grows up to be a singer whose earnings help build a skyscraper.

As you may have figured out by now, my parents were first cousins. Their families had made the match. Both of them had been sickly as children. They both liked the arts. And of course their families were already together, knew each other, and looked out for each other. That's how marriages were made in those days.

My parents got married in 1919. My father was working in Uncle Demetri's grocery store, and they lived with his family, too. That's where my older sister, Mary, was born in 1920, and my older brother, John, was born in 1923.

The number of children in all of the families was growing, and around this time my grandfather Antonio Suraci had decided that he wanted to live in a house with a garden that could one day be a center for the family. It was his dream, he told my grandmother: they should start to save for a house in the country.

Grandma Suraci said, "You want to live in a house? With a garden?" She got up, pulled out the trunk below their bed, and counted out $10,000 in small, soiled bills he had gotten from people who sold apples and melons from pushcarts. Grandpa Antonio was astonished. Ten thousand dollars in those days was like winning the lottery. Except, of course, Grandmother and Grandfather Suraci had earned each and every penny.

They found a house "in the country"—which in those days was Queens. A two-story house on 32nd Street. The train from Manhattan ran there (in the days before cars became widespread, "the country" had to be near a rail line), but there were still empty lots, including one next to the Suracis' house, where my grandmother kept her garden, a goat, and chickens.

Most of the rest of the Suracis and Benedettos followed them to Astoria, Queens, and the neighborhood into which I would be brought home in 1926 (the first in our family to be born in a hospital, St. John's Hospital in Long Island City). Queens seemed dramatically different from the teeming streets of Little Italy. We had trees, grass, and a garden, sunlight and blue sky.

And Queens is where we really entered America, because the people in Queens were from all around the world.

My father was already growing sicker and weaker by the time I was born, and he found it difficult to work. My parents moved into an apartment on Van Alst Avenue and Clark Street. It was my childhood apartment, the place in which I grew up, and I suppose I could almost walk blindfolded through it now if I had to. It was a second-floor, four-room "railroad flat," as they were called, the rooms lined up in a row like railroad cars (in some places, such a layout is called a "shotgun apartment" because you could fire a shot through the front door and it would zip, room by room, out the back door over the alley).

Our front door opened into the kitchen, which had a coal stove that was the only source of heat. The table was where we ate our meals, played cards and board games, and spent our time together. There was a small room off the kitchen with a small tub. That was where we washed our dishes and took our baths. The toilet was to the left of the washroom and was the only room in the apartment with a door. Behind the kitchen were my parents' bedroom, then my sister's bedroom, and finally the small living room, where my brother and I slept on a foldout couch. I can still remember how cold it got, four rooms away from the stove.

But I remember a lot of warmth more. Sunday afternoons, after church, all of the families in our extended family would go to my grandparents' house on 32nd Street. We'd open the door and find the dinner table practically groaning with platters of antipasto, steaming bowls of Calabrian minestrone with cabbage, beans, and cauliflower, and pasta with rich red tomato sauce. Then maybe a roast pork or chicken dish, fragrant with garlic, or a fish from the market, baked crispy, and bowls of sautéed tomatoes, zucchini, potatoes, and spinach. Then a parade of desserts, with torta della nonna, panna cotta, and half a dozen different kinds of cookies passed around the table.

Then the show would begin. The adults would take out their mandolins and guitars and sit in a circle. My sister, Mary, would be the mistress of ceremonies. My brother, Johnny, would sing. And me? I was the comedian in those days. I wish I could remember a single so-called joke I told. I think when you're the youngest kid, almost anything you say can be funny. I did love to hear the applause.

One of the greatest gifts my grandfather gave us by moving to Astoria, Queens, was to make us part of the whole wonderful and amazing mix of America. We were still proud Italian Americans. But we didn't live in Little Italy. We lived next door to, worshipped next to, shopped with, worked alongside, and got to know Jewish, Polish, Irish, and Greek families and, in time, some African American families, too. We went to Jewish delis and loved pastrami. Jews came to Italian restaurants and loved pasta e fagioli. The Irish kids learned Italian curse words, and the Greek kids sang along with all of us to Louis Armstrong's "Jeepers Creepers."

When I was a young singing waiter at Riccardo's restaurant under the Triborough Bridge, Irish families would come in and ask me to sing "As I Roved Out" or "I'll Take You Home Again,

Monet Garden #3

Kathleen." I'd tell them, "Be right back" and whisk back to the kitchen to ask the Irish waiters. They would give me a quick lesson and send me back to the dining room with the song they had taught me on my lips.

I don't want the years to leave me with too rosy a recollection. I'm sure all that diversity sometimes created tensions, too. But Queens prepared me to live in modern America like no other place. It helped me see the importance of not only tolerating differences but welcoming all kinds of people as part of the great wealth of America.

Not least, there was the skyline of Manhattan always in the distance. We knew that Manhattan was a kind of City of Gold. I spent hours looking at that skyline and dreaming. But never would I have dreamed they would light up the Empire State Building for me on my ninetieth birthday. But we also knew that the people of Queens, rising early, riding into town, and working late made that golden city work.

I've lived in Manhattan for most of my adult life, but I still get back to Queens. One reason is that there you can find the best food in New York; unlike pricey Manhattan places, the restaurants in Queens depend on repeat customers to survive.

My wife, Susan Benedetto, and I established Frank Sinatra School of the Arts in Astoria, Queens, a New York City public school with nearly a thousand students who get diplomas in fine art, dance, music, drama, and film. They put on musicals each year that could open on Broadway, and they have gone on to some of the greatest colleges in America, including Queens College's Aaron Copland School of Music, NYU's Tisch School of the Arts, Columbia, Amherst, Brigham Young, Cornell, and the Parsons School of Design.

Today, my blessed home borough of Queens is more urban

and even more diverse than it was when I was a boy. Families from Korea, China, Pakistan, Bangladesh, El Salvador, Colombia, India, Mexico, and dozens more countries have arrived over the past three generations, adding to the Irish, Italian, and Polish families, African Americans, Greeks, Jews, and so many others. It was important for us for the school to be in Queens to show that the arts are open to all the peoples of the world—as Astoria is.

Wherever I go in the world today, I am proudly a native New Yorker and a son of Astoria, Queens. Queens showed me that I had a place in the larger world. I am heartened to think that the school we've founded can make us part of the future of Queens, too.

The Metropolitan Museum

27

Abraham Lincoln

asn't every American been influenced by Abraham
Lincoln? He ended slavery, won the Civil War, and
remade America. Growing up in Queens during the
Great Depression, our immigrant Italian family (and a lot of
other families, Italian, Irish, Polish, Jewish, or African American) loved FDR, Eleanor Roosevelt, Fiorello La Guardia, and
Joe DiMaggio. But we learned about Lincoln in school and in
our families.

He had the very face of America. Lincoln's face is as much
a feature of the country as the mountains and the prairies are.
Look at his famous portraits by Mathew Brady, taken in the
days when you had to pose, frozen in place, for twenty minutes.
He looks serious, sad, noble, hardworking, and caring.

I became interested in the life of Lincoln over the years.
There is so much to be learned from him about generosity,
sacrifice, and for that matter humor. But Lincoln also reminds
those of us who are performers (and at some point in our lives
all of us will be, whether to make a classroom report or sales

presentation or sing at La Scala) about the value of brevity, or what Gypsy Rose Lee is often credited with saying: "Always leave them wanting more."

Everyone knows about Lincoln's Gettysburg Address. When I was a schoolkid, a lot of us even memorized it. What we remember less about that November 19, 1863, dedication of the Soldiers' National Cemetery in Gettysburg is that Edward Everett, the most famous and admired orator of his time, preceded Lincoln and spoke for two hours. Lincoln spoke for two minutes.

Almost every American knows at least a phrase or two of the Gettysburg Address: "Four score and seven years ago . . . The world will little note, nor long remember what we say here, but it can never forget what they did here . . . that government of the people, by the people, for the people, shall not perish from the earth."

Can any of us remember a single phrase poor Edward Everett spoke that day?

Over the years, I'd read the works of a man named Harold Holzer, who wrote a lot about Lincoln. When I realized that he had an office in New York, I looked him up, and we became friends. Harold edited a book on Lincoln with Mario Cuomo and consulted on Steven Spielberg's great film *Lincoln*. He has helped me understand that Edward Everett was an admirable guy, not just a blowhard. He served as the US secretary of state, senator from Massachusetts, and president of Harvard. People traveled for hours and days to get to Gettysburg for the event. They booked Edward Everett for the cemetery dedication gig, if you please, precisely to put on a two-hour show of oratory that would make it worth the trip.

President Lincoln was busy running the war. He was always

just supposed to make a few remarks to end the dedication, not to be the featured performance.

Edward Everett began, "Standing beneath this serene sky, overlooking these broad fields now reposing from the labors of the waning year, the mighty Alleghenies dimly towering before us, the graves of our brethren beneath our feet . . ."

It's a good beginning. But it would take another minute to reach the end of just his first sentence.

What Abe Lincoln did in the Gettysburg Address had something in common with a great song (a great *short* song, I might dare to put it). He begins with a phrase that draws you in ("Four score and seven years ago") and puts what follows into a rolling tide of a story. He sets up a rhythm and cadence ("But, in a larger sense, we cannot dedicate—we cannot consecrate—we cannot hallow—this ground") on his way to the shattering end ("shall not perish from the earth").

Then he leaves the stage while people are still leaning forward and listening.

Historians disagree about whether the audience in attendance at Gettysburg truly understood that they had heard a great speech from Lincoln, much less one of the great speeches of history. The *New York Times*' account of that day says he was interrupted by applause five times and got long, sustained applause when he was done. But its report is sometimes dismissed as partisan (the *Times* was considered a Republican paper in those days, a long time ago). Other news accounts were pretty withering.

A lot of eyewitnesses who were there told various historians over the years that the crowd had been hushed. Some said it was because they were unmoved; others said it was because they were so deeply moved. The historian Shelby Foote says in his great Civil War trilogy that Lincoln received only "barely polite" applause.

But Edward Everett was an astute man who realized instantly that Lincoln's two minutes had stolen the show. He wrote the president the next day, "I should be glad if I could flatter myself that I came as near to the central idea of the occasion, in two hours, as you did in two minutes."

Everett was a good man who did not make it to the end of the war. He caught a very bad cold while speaking to a crowd in Boston to raise money for the poor of Savannah, a southern city that General William Tecumseh Sherman's Union troops had recently won for the North. He died a few days later, at the age of seventy.

Anyone can learn from Lincoln's enormous largeness of spirit. Those of us who are performers can look at the public utterance for which he is best remembered and take our own cue from Abe Lincoln: Don't feel that you have to show people everything you can do. Just show them the best you can do.

Boy on Sailboat

Taormina, Sicily

Jack Benny and George Burns

J ack Benny and George Burns gave me the wisest, truest advice about show business that I probably ever heard. But it took me seven or eight years to know they were right.

It was sometime in 1952. I'd had two of my first big hits the year before. "Because of You" had reached number one on the pop charts, followed up by a rendition of Hank Williams's beautiful, bittersweet "Cold, Cold Heart," which also hit the charts. I was booked into the Paramount Theatre on Broadway, where the shows were sold out.

I saw Jack and George walking down Broadway one afternoon. They were often together in the public mind even then, devoted friends who saw or talked to each other each day, no matter where they were or what they were working on.

Both Jack and George had enjoyed successful radio shows, which they were beginning to bring to television. Their shows were among the first sitcoms. They costarred with their spouses (Mary Livingstone, Jack's wife, who was born Sadie Marks, and Gracie Allen, who of course was married to George), and the episodes were often set in their television "homes." So it was easy to confuse the violin-strangling Jack Benny of his show and the cigar-brandishing George Burns of Burns and Allen with the real-life people behind those names. If you saw them on the street, you'd think you were running into old friends.

But they were also the biggest names in broadcasting at that point. I didn't want to be like just another fan when I saw them walking together, so I looked away. But Jack and George stopped me on the sidewalk and said, "Congratulations, kid, you're doing pretty well." I thanked them, of course, and was enormously flattered. But then they looked at me with shrewd eyes and said, "It'll take you seven or eight years to know what you're really doing."

That left me a little puzzled at the time. "Because of You" had sold more than a million copies. I was doing six or seven shows a day, all of them sold out, at one of Broadway's best houses. Wouldn't almost anyone kind of have to say that I pretty much already knew what I was doing?

But Jack and George were shrewd in the ways of both show business and life. They had become such well-known characters on radio and TV that millions of Americans felt they were practically members of the family.

Jack was the guy who held his face to exclaim surprise, fretted over pennies, kicked his coughing Maxwell motorcar, and claimed for decades to be just thirty-nine. George smiled slyly, waved his cigar like a wand, and generously teed up punch lines for his wife, Gracie. (And I love what he said about her: "She made me look talented, and I was—talented enough to be married to her for thirty-eight years.")

But it was easy to forget the hard work it had taken for them to get there. Jack Benny and George Burns were highly disci-

Garden, Buckingham Palace

plined professionals. Each had honed his craft on a thousand different vaudeville and nightclub stages across the country before they ever appeared on radio or television. (Jack, by the way, had to change his name from Benjamin Kubelsky because the great Czech violinist and composer Jan Kubelík didn't want to be confused with a young American vaudevillian who mostly played his violin for laughs.) They knew how to stride onstage and hold audiences in the palms of their hands. They knew how to get laughs and get off at just the right time, before the laughs could fade. They had learned, over years and years, how to create a personality onstage that sincerely reflected who they were, while also creating larger comic characters. Mostly, they had learned how to stay fresh and worth seeing year after year— after year.

And they never tired of making each other laugh or showing each other new ways to do it. They went to many Hollywood parties together, and at one, Jack turned to George and said, "This party is a bore. Tell you what: I'm going to go upstairs, take off my pants, and then come downstairs. Let's see what happens."

But when Jack whisked upstairs to take off his pants, George told the assembled partygoers what he planned to do. When Jack came downstairs, no one turned a head or batted an eye. And that made Jack break up laughing.

So something like eight years after I'd encountered those two wise men of comedy, Jack Benny and George Burns, on the street, I agreed to appear at a benefit at the Hollywood Bowl. They were on the bill, too, and I saw them sitting backstage, just talking. I had just recorded my albums with Count Basie and was proud of them. But seeing Jack and George there helped me realize how much I had learned in seven or eight years. I had been a young hotshot with a number one record who thought he knew it all. It took falling off the charts, making some mistakes, figuring out what were the best songs and how I could do them better, and learning, through trial and error, how to present a complete show, not just a few good songs, before I could look in the mirror and begin to see a real professional entertainer of the kind that I admired—like Jack Benny and George Burns.

They smiled when I went over to say hello and said, "We remember running into you a while back." I didn't remind them that "a while back" had been seven or eight years before. "You gave me some great advice," I told them, and I think George waved his cigar while one or the other of them said, "Us? Great advice? Impossible." But isn't that just what you'd expect Jack Benny and George Burns to say?

The Hills of Florence

Sammy Cahn

S ammy Cahn was my neighbor for a few years in California, and he used to tell me, "Drop over for a cup of song sometime." I sure did.

Sammy was a courtly gentleman who, with his writing partner and composer, Jimmy Van Heusen, was considered to be practically Frank Sinatra's personal songwriter. If you start remembering great Sinatra songs in any group of people, it will soon become a recollection of great Sammy Cahn and Jimmy Van Heusen songs, too. "Come Fly with Me," "All the Way"—don't you hear Frank's way with those phrases in your head as you read the titles? And then there was "Three Coins in the Fountain," which Sammy wrote with Jule Styne.

Sammy was another of the great New York songwriters who rolled out to Hollywood when movies were rolling out of the major studios and needed scores and songs done quickly. Sammy (who was born Sammy Cohen, but changed his name twice: to Kahn, to avoid being confused with an actor of the same name, and then to Cahn, because there was a lyricist named Gus

Kahn) was a talented pianist and violinist. He formed a small band to tour the Catskills shortly after his bar mitzvah, which he told me displeased his mother. She had hoped he would become a dignified classical musician, in white tie and tails.

Sammy wound up playing music in vaudeville houses and said the experience ingrained in him a feeling for a strong finish that would bring an audience to its feet. Sammy pointed to the refrain at the end of "Three Coins in a Fountain": "Make it mine, make it mine, make it mine!" and said, "Let people know they should applaud, and they will."

"Three Coins in a Fountain" won the Oscar for Best Original Song in 1954 (with Frank recording it, of course). Sammy teamed with Jimmy Van Heusen to follow with "Love and Marriage" in 1955, for a television production of Thornton Wilder's *Our Town* (also sung by Frank, who played the Stage Manager). Frank helped them to another huge hit when he recorded "Come Fly with Me" in 1957. The song perfectly captures the poetic excitement of the great age of air travel, the first big jets and the feeling of being free and soaring above the world. It's a romantic swing tune, but the stanzas soar from Bombay to Peru, and flying ("where the air is rarified"—a great internal rhyme) is half the fun of getting there. I particularly like the stanza, slightly racy, where Sammy wrote, "In llama land there's a one-man band / And he'll toot his flute for you."

They wrote "All the Way" for Frank to sing for the 1957 film *The Joker Is Wild*, in which Frank gives a strong performance as Joe E. Lewis, a real-life Chicago nightclub performer (and one of Frank's favorite drinking companions) who stood up to "Machine Gun" Jack McGurn of the Al Capone mob. "All the Way" has one of the smartest beginnings in popular song: "When somebody loves you / It's no good unless he loves you . . ." Then there's that slight pause in the roll of the words, a second of mystery and anticipation, before the end comes in: ". . . all the way!"

Sammy won four Oscars for "Three Coins in a Fountain," "All the Way," "High Hopes" (from the 1959 film *A Hole in the Head*—starring Frank Sinatra, too), and that beautiful ballad "Call Me Irresponsible" for the 1963 film *Papa's Delicate Condition* (Frank made a hit of it, of course, but the song was actually first sung by Jackie Gleason).

Sammy Cahn was nominated for twenty-six Oscars for Best Original Song in a span over thirty-two years. That's practically one a year. Almost any of the losers could have just as easily won, including "Come Blow Your Horn," "Love Is the Tender Trap," the piercing "The Second Time Around," and "My Kind of Town," the only part of the 1964 film *Robin and the 7 Hoods* that most anyone remembers. They were all Sinatra songs, too. Is there a pattern here?

Sammy was nominated for so many Oscars that songwriters wound up naming a songwriting award for movie songs "the Sammy Award."

"All the Way," "The Second Time Around," "Time After Time," and "My Kind of Town" are all standards in the music mix of how we live, and I sing them to this day. My old neighbor Sammy Cahn and his writing partners gave us all many beautiful "cups of song" to take through our lives.

Spring in Central Park

Al Jolson

The voice of Al Jolson was just about the first one I could identify. I heard him on the radio, on the *Dodge Victory Hour* and *Presenting Al Jolson*. His voice was rich, resonant, smooth, and spirited. Microphones were new, clumsy, and unreliable. Jolson still sang to the back row of one of the vast Broadway theaters that he filled to the rafters. His voice filled our living room and followed us into our bedrooms when we listened.

Jolson was one of the first people in America to be not only a household name but a household voice. His voice was as familiar to me as the speech of an aunt, an uncle, or a teacher.

My father loved Al Jolson. He took me to see *The Singing Fool* when I was about three. It was one of the first talkies (a singie, actually; the dialog between characters was still flashed onscreen, but the musical numbers were recorded). I was swept away by Jolson, who sang "Sonny Boy" in the film. That Sunday, while my parents entertained all my aunts, uncles, and cousins, I crept into their bedroom and patted some of my mother's powder onto my face. Then I leaped into the living room. "Me Sonny Boy!" I announced, and hearing my whole family laugh and clap was my first real taste of applause.

It's hard to understand, in this day and age, the hold that Al Jolson had on American entertainment. He was the biggest stage performer in the United States (he had nine straight sold-out shows at the Winter Garden), the biggest radio and recording star (more than eighty hit records), and the first real singing movie star (*The Jazz Singer* transformed movies when it came out in 1927), all at the same time. It's hard to see Jolson for the great entertainer he was, above, beyond, and below the blackface he wore for a few of his most famous songs.

Al was born Asa Yoelson in what is now Lithuania. His father was a cantor, who was able to move to New York shortly after Al was born. But he couldn't bring Al and the rest of his family over for almost five years. And within that first year in America, Al's mother died. He grew up depressed, grieving, and angry and spent a couple of years in the same orphanage and reformatory in Baltimore where Babe Ruth had been as a boy.

Al and his brother, Harry, began to sing on street corners for change to support themselves. In time, Al began to audition for stage shows, and audiences had never seen a performer so energetic, generous, and electric. His joy leaped across the stage and into the aisles. He often leaned down to sing to people in their seats. He totally immersed himself in the performance of a song, sweating, shivering, and tearing up. He chose songs—"My Mammy," "Sonny Boy"—that tugged at the heart, and he sang them in an open, emotional style that made grown men and women sob with thoughts of the love they'd never quite had the chance or nerve to express.

In our times, Al Jolson's use of blackface has obscured a lot of his greatness with a continuing controversy. It's not something that any performer would or should do today. But in the 1920s, blackface was a theatrical convention, almost like wearing a mask in a Greek drama. It was thought to give performers a sense of freedom and liberation if they did not have to look like themselves. A lot of critics even thought that blackface acts were a form of tribute to black culture and history. Al Jolson's stage persona in blackface was wise and talented, not comically slow or stupid, the way a lot of other caricatures by whites of blacks were at the time.

And in fact, Al loved jazz, blues, and ragtime, the music he had learned and admired from black performers who were his friends (including the great Bill "Bojangles" Robinson, Eubie Blake, and Cab Calloway). He brought that music onstage before millions. Al opposed segregation and insisted on equal pay for black performers in his stage shows. In fact, there were critics who found in Al Jolson's blackface an expression of solidarity from a Jewish man, a cantor's son, who had also known the sting of segregation.

Hearing and seeing Al Jolson were probably my first glimpse of what a life in show business could be like, and it inspired me. As I've grown older and endured my own ups and downs, I've found something else to admire in Al Jolson, too.

Jolson's career went through dips in the 1930s and '40s. There's no business like show business, and no business more fickle. New songs come out every week. There's a new hit parade and top ten every week. Cool crooners, such as Bing, Frank, and Nat, had become popular, and Al's style was classic, not contemporary. He was so expressive, he was easy to mock, and though he continued to work, he felt he was being left behind.

But when Pearl Harbor was bombed, Al went on the road to entertain US troops, even before the USO was created, and at his own expense. He sang and danced his heart out for soldiers stationed from Alaska to Ireland and back to Central America, and practically stopped traffic in London when he arrived, unheralded, with some of the first US troops and put on a show. Al told the *New York Times*, "I felt like I needed to do something for our boys, and all I knew was show business."

Al was touring bases in the Pacific in 1945 when he contracted malaria. He had to have his left lung taken out, but he kept on singing.

Al earned the admiration of a whole new generation. In 1946, *The Jolson Story* movie came out, with Larry Parks playing Al. But Al sang the movie's songs, and even appeared, from a distance, performing "Swanee" all over again. He was as magnetic and energetic as ever, at the age of sixty and singing and acting on one lung. Larry Parks, who did a fine job playing, if not singing, for Jolson, said he lost nineteen pounds just trying to act like Al for the few weeks of shooting.

The movie was a huge hit, won lots of awards, and spawned a demand for an immediate sequel. Al was back in demand. He was back on top.

Here's what I think we should learn from Al Jolson's example: do the best you can do, and trust that an audience will respect that and find you. Al didn't try to imitate the new talents as they came along. That would have been inauthentic and, in the end, unsuccessful. He stayed true to himself, and new audiences found themselves drawn to him. They wanted to see the great Jolson, not some Crosby-Sinatra-Cole imitator.

I hope I've had the same kind of integrity Al did as a performer when producers and executives tried to persuade me to do material that I knew wasn't right for me—wasn't the best that I could do.

The Korean War came along in 1950. Al called President Harry Truman to ask him to let him go overseas to entertain the new, young US soldiers called into action. When some White House functionary told him that the USO had been disbanded after World War II, Al barked, "I've got funds. I'll pay myself," and he did. He did forty-two shows for US soldiers in Korea over sixteen days.

Jolson had to get back to the United States because he had signed, after all those years, to star in a new film, about a USO troupe during World War II. But the journey to Korea and all the shows there had taxed a man in his sixties—even Al Jolson—who was working on one lung. He had a heart attack in his hotel suite in San Francisco and died at the age of sixty-four.

The lights of Broadway were dimmed in Al's honor, and tributes were broadcast all over the world. I can't help but think that the one that would have meant the most to him was a bridge in Korea over which US soldiers had to pass to get back from the front lines; it was renamed the Al Jolson Bridge.

Homage to Hockney

31

Duke Ellington

D uke Ellington used to send me roses: gorgeous long-stemmed pink roses (he didn't stint on elegance) whenever he had a song he wanted me to hear. And he signed off on all of his cards, telegrams, and phone calls, "Love you madly." I sure did, right back.

Duke wrote more than a thousand compositions, and I wish I'd had the time to record all of them (that would have been a lot of roses). His creativity was ceaseless, constant, and unquenchable.

Duke's often been compared to Beethoven or Puccini, for the elegant intricacy of his compositions. I also think of Picasso and his restless, almost compulsive inventiveness. Creativity never comes easy. But Duke's genius was unstoppable.

It's amazing to think—but important not to forget—that when Duke and I were the first performers to open Miami's Americana Hotel in 1956, Duke couldn't attend the press party. It was Florida, it was the South, and the hotel was segregated. Any white man with 50 cents in his pocket could buy a beer at the bar. But the creative genius who brought in customers by the thousands couldn't sit next to him. That was America then.

But I also remember the time Duke confided an old trick to me: When he was on tour, he'd book a penthouse suite for his band manager, who was white, in the best hotel in town. Then the manager would give Duke his key. Duke, his long-time collaborator Billy Strayhorn, and a couple of other featured bandmates would sleep soundly there. And when Duke's band traveled through the South, they'd book private train cars in which they'd sleep, eat, and even rehearse. They essentially glided over the abhorrent laws of segregation.

Duke was such a prolific composer that no one or two lyric writers could keep up with him. Typically, he'd write a song as an instrumental, his band would make it part of its repertoire, and it would already be a hit by the time Duke could find a lyricist to add words.

One of my favorite songs to sing of Duke's is "Don't Get Around Much Anymore," which he wrote as an instrumental in 1940. Bob Russell added lyrics in 1942, and I'm glad he did. It's a sprightly tune that turns into a wistful melody for a love that didn't last—but, hey, that's life.

Thought I'd visit the club / Got as far as the door . . .

It's a ditty, not a dirge. Duke's song had the stamp of wisdom and the experience of knowing that something and someone else would come along.

Duke was born in Washington, DC, the nation's capital, but still a southern city, especially the year of his birth, in 1899. In fact, Duke's mother, Daisy, was the daughter of a slave. His father, James, made blueprints for the Department of the Navy in DC. Both parents played the piano, and Duke learned from them.

A piano was not just a fixture in their home but the family entertainment system. Duke learned to play classical music, standards, hymns, and spirituals, without any sense that one kind of music was more or less sophisticated than another. Duke always used to tell me, "There's only good music and bad music."

I've been asked many times, "What made Duke Ellington so great?" and I always make a point of telling people "You can hear it for yourself. But you have to begin with Duke's mother. Duke said she always told him, 'You are great. You are a gift to the world,' and made him a believer in that, too."

Edward Kennedy Ellington told me he almost couldn't remember a time that he wasn't called Duke. He carried himself with dapper elegance and courtly manners, even as a kid. The name Duke just seemed to suit him—much more than Ed.

Duke began to play clubs and cafés in Washington from the time he was a teenager. He once worked behind the counter at a place called the Poodle Dog Café that already had a piano player. But the pianist often had too much to drink too early in the day. That's when the owner would say, "Duke, take over," and Duke would hang up his apron, slip on a jacket, and play. Duke was fourteen when he completed his first full composition (known today as the "Soda Fountain Rag," or sometimes "Poodle Dog Rag"), which he said he wrote to capture all the spritzing, spraying, and squirting he'd do behind the counter.

Duke was also a talented artist who had turned down an art scholarship to the Pratt Institute and begun his own sign-painting business. ("Don't do just one thing," Duke always told me, which inspired me to work at my painting, too.) But when a client would hire him to draw a sign for some kind of dance party, Duke would offer to be the entertainment. He began to make a reputation more for his music than for his artwork. His first group was called "The Duke's Serenaders" (their listing in the DC yellow pages billed them as "Colored Syncopaters"), and in segregated Washington, Duke's became the orchestra of choice at numerous embassy parties, debutante balls, and birthdays.

Duke moved to New York in the 1920s. He had a comfortable slot in Washington society but didn't want to play just for embassy parties, and he wanted to find a place in Harlem's Cultural Renaissance. In a short time, he formed the house band at Harlem's Cotton Club, and soon thereafter he won a name for the weekly national radio broadcasts from the club.

Duke led his band more by inspiration and example than direction. He conducted from the keyboard, not a podium. He'd lift an eyebrow or his hand for a cue and see to it that each member of the orchestra had a moment to improvise and shine in the course of a performance.

When the Great Depression struck, millions of Americans were staggered and suffering. The music of Duke Ellington lifted them up. It had verve, lilt, and swing and reminded them of America's strength, vigor, and inventiveness. "It Don't Mean a Thing (If It Ain't Got That Swing)" came in 1932, "Sophisticated Lady" in 1933, "In a Sentimental Mood" in 1935.

"Sophisticated Lady" is one of the great American songs of all time. Adelaide Hall did a knockout version on the original recording, and all of the greatest American female vocalists—Billie Holiday, Sarah Vaughan, Ella Fitzgerald, Julie London, and in recent times Linda Ronstadt and the great Natalie Cole—have recorded versions. It turns out to be one of Lady Gaga's favorite songs, cool and shrewdly observerd. The Lady and I did our own on our 2014 duets album. Mitchell Parish wrote the lyrics to Duke's luxurious melody, and the song is a kind of ballad to people who laugh on the outside while they carry a torch inside their heart:

Smoking, drinking
Never thinking of tomorrow . . .

Duke said the people who inspired the song in his mind were not Manhattan swells, but a few grade school teachers he had in DC who would go off to Europe during their summer break. That seemed the height of sophistication when he was a kid.

It's hard to appreciate sometimes how much of American music runs through Duke Ellington's work. He and his band were on break while playing at the Lincoln Tavern in Chicago in 1931, and during the intermission, when most people would have been napping, drinking, or smoking, Duke was writing a composition. (I told you: he was ceaselessly creative. He couldn't just rest, like most people. He had to have something to show for it!) One of Duke's great gifts was to appreciate and incorporate the talents, thoughts, and feelings of his bandmates into his music. He wrote a composition around the words that were the credo of his trumpet player, Bubber Miley: "It don't mean a thing if it ain't got that swing." He may have been the man who coined that word for the music that was setting hearts racing and toes tapping all over America.

Bubber, by the way, had tuberculosis and didn't live to see the song recorded, with Johnny Hodges on sax and Ivie Anderson singing those great lyrics by Irving Mills: "It makes no difference if it's sweet or hot / Just give that rhythm everything you've got."

Duke became a big name in Europe and began to tour there. The name Duke Ellington became, almost like Coca-Cola, a symbol of America. The British and French in particular praised his longer orchestral pieces, including *Creole Rhapsody* in 1931, and *Reminiscing in Tempo*, a tribute Duke wrote for his mother after she died in 1935. That work took up four sides of a ten-inch record, and although mostly shorter versions are available on CD and download today, it's well worth hearing. It's touching and lilting and captures the spirit of a young mother who cherished her son and gave him to the world.

Duke Ellington was a genius. He was unfailingly courteous and generous, but he kept to himself a lot. Who else could understand the depth of what went on inside his brilliant mind? We spent a lot of time together over the years; we talked about music and musicians and traded stories about producers, club owners, and friends. But Duke rarely talked about himself. He even wrote his music around the various talents of his bandmates, whom he knew so well. In 1956, he made a historic appearance at the Newport Jazz Festival, where the saxophonist Paul Gonsalves played a twenty-seven-chorus solo in the middle of Duke's "Diminuendo and Crescendo in Blue" that became the center of the best-selling LP of Duke's career.

For all of his acclaim, Duke was unassuming about himself. But he could be supremely demonstrative in friendship.

The Christmas season of 1965 was the worst that I'd lived through since the time I was ten and my father died. My wife, Patricia, and I had split up. I wasn't welcome at our family home in New Jersey, and I missed my two sons. I was living in a small, spiritless room in the Gotham Hotel and felt sad, depressed, and lonely, yet too embarrassed to admit that to anybody and ask for companionship or cheer. For me the season was cold and gray.

One day during the holiday season, I heard singing in the hotel hallway. I figured the singers were carolers who wanted a contribution for a good cause, and I threw open the door. I saw about a dozen singers in the hallway. They were singing the Alan Jay Lerner and Burton Lane song "On a Clear Day You Can See Forever." It turned out that Duke was giving a concert of sacred music at a church on Fifth Avenue. Louis Bellson, his drummer, told Duke that I was low. So he sent over a choir of voices to cheer me up. I invited them in, and we sang together, making the holiday for me, courtesy of Duke.

Duke wasn't a person to explain himself much. He didn't speak a lot about his spiritual life. He just lived it. He used to say that the only book he'd read cover to cover was the Bible. And he believed it was the only book you really needed to read.

"Tony," he said, "it can get boiled down to a single message, like a great song: God is love." Of all the paintings I've done, my favorite is a portrait of Duke, which I was thrilled to give to the National Portrait Gallery in Washington, DC. I called it *Duke Ellington: "God Is Love."* He tried to live by that, too.

Today Duke Ellington is on a stamp, his name is on schools, and he's hailed as a genius. But we should remind ourselves that Duke, and every other entertainer doing the great songs we believed in, including me, got hit hard by the rise of rock in the '50s and '60s. The folks who ran the record companies would anoint some new young talent or group and promote the hell out of them—for a few months or a year. Just take a look at *Billboard*'s top songs of 1962. You'll see some names and songs that have stood the test of time, such as the peerless Elvis Presley, the Shirelles, Neil Sedaka, and the great Ray Charles. But you'll also see a lot of one- or two-hit wonders, like Joey Dee and the Starliters, and Bobby (Boris) Pickett and the Crypt-Kickers (who recorded that timeless "classic" "Monster Mash").

Record company executives were always eager to "discover" new young talent (and to be sure, a lot of them were talented; I don't want to sound like some scolding old fool who doesn't think anything good has been written since Frank Sinatra sent bobby-soxers into a swoon). The record companies could direct, mold, and ultimately own new young talent in a way they couldn't order around established artists who had built their own identity, such as Duke Ellington, Frank Sinatra, and Ella Fitzgerald. And, I hope, me.

Duke said he was once summoned to a meeting with Columbia Records executives who cleared their throats, cracked their knuckles, and announced, "Uh, oh, sorry, Duke, but your records just aren't selling the way they used to." That was after they had done almost nothing to promote his new records, just relying on Duke's stellar name.

"I guess I must be mistaken," Duke said he told the execs. "I thought I was supposed to make the records and you were supposed to sell them."

That sharp observation reminds me to this day that everything I need to know about the music business can be found in the Bible of Duke Ellington.

Duke and I did twenty-five concerts with the New York Philharmonic in 1968, to mark my twenty years in show business. I took second billing. The only time I had ever done that before was with Count Basie and Frank Sinatra. I have no problem playing second bill to royalty—Duke, the Count, or the Chairman of the Board. They have elevated me in every way.

I think what I learned most from Duke over the decades was how his extraordinary creative output was so original and distinct, he never worried about going into or out of style. He was always Duke, his own man, with that singular, inimitable style that belonged to no one else and was matched by no one else. He didn't look at the weekly hit parade or the year's *Billboard* rankings. He took the long view, as all great artists do. Some years would be better than others. But in the end, they all added up to an unsurpassed life and career.

I have a favorite image of Duke that I keep in my mind. Bobby Hackett and I were playing the Somerset Hotel in Boston in the early '60s, and one bright day we were sitting in my room or Bobby's room when the phone rang. It was Duke. He said to come down to the lobby, there was a piano and he wanted us to hear a song. It was a broken-down old relic of a piano, with eight notes on the middle C octave busted. But Duke played it anyway, for an hour, choosing notes that would avoid that octave.

Duke Ellington found a new way to make an old piano play the music that flowed from his soul into his fingers. His creativity was ceaseless, restless, and tireless. We have a whole world of music to see us through our lives because of him.

Il Duomo, Florence

32

John Singer Sargent

I've always thought a singer has certain things in common with a portrait painter. Each of us is entrusted with something that is precious. A portrait painter is asked to capture a person's appearance in a way that conveys his character and spirit. A singer is asked to perform a song in a way that captures what the composer wants to say and wants others to feel. But there are no guarantees written into the relationship between the song or subject and an artist or the public.

I sometimes think of this when I look at the works of John Singer Sargent. Over the years, he has become my favorite painter and the one from whom I have learned the most (if you can truly learn from a genius). But that may be as much about music as art.

Singer is often considered the greatest portrait painter of his time and more. I got to know his works through my friend Everett Raymond Kinstler. Ev is often considered the greatest American portrait painter of our time, so he ought to know. Ev happened to go to New York's School of Industrial Art at the same time I did, though we wouldn't meet until years later.

Sargent was born in 1856 to American parents who were living in Florence, Italy, a couple of years after they lost their two-year-old daughter to a fatal illness. Young John was identified as a prodigy at drawing, languages, music, and literature. Every artist his parents engaged to teach him about fine art said that he wound up learning from him. They were flabbergasted to see his early mastery of line, color, and the portrayal of light.

Sargent began by painting landscapes and seascapes, not portraits. But pictures of beaches, waves, forests, and mountains have to be painted in the hope that they'll eventually be bought by someone. Portraits are commissioned in advance. They're paid for before an artist even picks up his brush—and that sounds good to a struggling young artist. Sargent, who was shrewd, charming, and fluent in most of the languages of Europe, soon had clients practically lining up to be painted by him.

Perhaps his most famous portrait was *Portrait of Madame X*, which he completed in 1884. Madame X was Virginie Amélie Avegno, a beauty who had been born in America, come to France as a young socialite, and married Pierre Gautreau, a famous and powerful banker. Madame's beauty was heralded and renowned. Her hair was russet; she had the neck and profile of an elegant swan, and a full, shapely figure. There were no paparazzi in those days, but many artists lusted to paint Madame Gautreau.

Don't let anyone tell you there's anything new about celebrity. Madame Gautreau was one of her era's beauties, the object of scandalous speculation, the image of dreams, and the cause of shattered hearts.

She did not commission Sargent to paint her portrait. But he was among the artists who pursued her, and he sent word through a mutual friend that he would be the best painter to produce what he called an "homage to her beauty. If you are 'bien avec elle'"—a phrase that essentially means "on good terms with the lady,"—"and will see her in Paris, you might tell her I am a man of prodigious talent."

She succumbed to Singer's artistic overtures. The Madame, as much as the painter, wanted to wow Paris society.

The sittings were reportedly long and arduous for Sargent, long and tedious for Madame Gautreau. Singer produced at least thirty studies in pencil and watercolor before beginning the portrait in oil (a few studies are now on display at Boston's Isabella Stewart Gardner Museum). Madame did not like spending hours sitting on a couch or standing in a heavy velvet dress in front of a window, turning only an inch or two to catch another sliver of light while Sargent laid down another line or a wash of color. She had lunches and parties to attend, houseguests, staff, and a young daughter. But she made the time in the expectation that it would produce a masterpiece that would stand for the ages as a testament to her beauty.

I think it does just that. Madame Gautreau is shown in a way that both draws the eye to her famous, graceful profile and boldly presents the hourglass figure, powerful arms, majestic, milky white shoulders, and sinuous curves that figured in a thousand dreams. She is painted in a rich brown dress against a burnished tobacco brown background, which lets the flesh exposed by her dress shine. It was not the way one expected to see a contemporary woman painted for public display in the 1880s.

In the original painting, Madame's left dress strap has slipped down. Showing a dress strap that had slipped off of a woman's shoulder was considered scandalous in 1884. Even in Paris. It suggested to some eyes that the dress was about to come off. Why? For whom?

Madame Gautreau applied lavender powder to her skin, and to capture her singular tone, Sargent concocted his own distinctive mix of bone black, lead white, rose, viridian, and vermilion. No printing technique, even today, can quite do justice to that color. But her right ear is unpowdered and pink, perhaps to reveal that Madame put every inch of herself together.

According to art historians, Madame Gautreau loved the painting while it was being done. It seemed to be the masterpiece she felt she deserved. But then it was presented, with great flourish, at the famous Salon de Paris, the official exhibit space of the Académie des Beaux-Arts. The critics howled. They decried the portrait as brazen, graphic, and seamy. More to the point, Madame Gautreau's *mother* was mortified and asked Sargent to withdraw the painting, which he refused to do. But he did go back to his canvas and repainted the right strap so that it was affixed over her shoulder.

Madame Gautreau said she was scandalized. She didn't remain *Madame X* for long. She was too famously and distinctively beautiful (and, I'll bet, in the end more delighted than disgraced by all the attention). Sargent felt misunderstood and wound up moving to London to continue his stellar career.

Several other great portrait painters, including Gustave Courtois, would go on to paint Madame Gautreau, and their results were more to her liking. It's worth it to take a look at Courtois's 1891 painting *Madame Gautreau* (no *X* required at that point). It exhibits almost as much of Madame's skin, except that her dress is white, without the sensational contrast of the brown dress and bronze backdrop. But even Courtois shows her left shoulder strap down, perhaps in homage to Singer's singular artistry.

John Singer Sargent went on to become one of the great portrait painters of all time, his portraits of so many of the great figures of London society, royals, writers, artists, Rockefellers, Vanderbilts, and two US presidents, Teddy Roosevelt and Woodrow Wilson, commanding unprecedented prices and public notice. He would paint about a dozen portraits a year and also painted the landscapes and seascapes that he loved and that I love to look at today.

Still, Sargent considered a portrait to be a work of art, not commerce. It was a wild thing that had a life of its own, as art does. He would paint a portrait to try to capture someone's spirit or character. But Sargent couldn't guarantee that the way he saw that person would reflect the way he or she saw him- or herself. The wisest people he painted would know it was an honor to have the master do their portrait.

Sargent's memory of his *Madame X* might have been on his mind when he wrote, "Every time I paint a portrait I lose a friend." In the end, the artist has to come down on the side of art.

In some ways, singers have to have that audacity, too. They sing a song the way they hear it inside their hearts. They welcome what a composer tells them about what's in there, but the best songwriters know and are eager to accept what a great singer can discover in their notes and words that maybe even they didn't know was there. The different discoveries by different voices are what makes a song a classic that stands the test of time and sound as interesting the thousandth time you hear it as the first or second time.

Today, I love to look at portraits by John Singer Sargent of people whom I know only by that portrait, and landscapes and seascapes that have long ago disappeared. Singer's artistry makes them alive for me and renews them in my eyes. Those of us who have to sing for a living have to keep the great songs alive the same way.

Sunday in Central Park

Ella Fitzgerald

When I asked my mother where she'd like to be taken for her birthday in 1952, I was delighted (and a little surprised) to hear her say, "Birdland! I want to see Ella Fitzgerald."

My mother always knew quality.

We were seated at a ringside table, and after her show Ella came out over our drinks and introduced herself. I stood up for the Queen of Jazz, and she told me, "I loved your recording of 'Blue Velvet.'"

I felt as if I had been knighted—right in front of my mother.

Ella was an astounding musician, as well as a great singer. Her voice was her instrument. It was clear and fresh as a silver bell, with flawless, note-perfect phrasing, tremendous power and range, and often astounding delicacy.

"I never knew how good our songs were," Ira Gershwin said so memorably, "until I heard Ella Fitzgerald sing them."

But the Queen of Jazz did not have royal beginnings.

Ella was born in Newport News, Virginia, to her mother,

Temperance, and a man named William Fitzgerald. Her mother later left her father and took up with a new boyfriend within a few months. They moved to Yonkers, New York. Young Ella was active in her Methodist church choir and Bible study group. She loved dance classes and began to tap-dance in school shows. She heard a lot of radio and a lot of jazz and fell for Louis Armstrong, Bing Crosby, and Connee Boswell, a great Kansas City singer from the 1930s who did a number of big duets with Bing.

Then Ella's mother died suddenly when Ella was fifteen, and life became difficult for her until she entered an amateur night at Harlem's Apollo Theater. She'd planned to dance when her turn was called, but several dancers had gone before her and she worried that her dancing might not make an impression.

Amateur night at the Apollo could be rough on young talents. The audience booed freely when people came onstage who seemed uncomfortable, scared, or unprepared. Ella thought of Connee Boswell's recording of "Judy," a Hoagy Carmichael/Sammy Lerner song she loved, and asked the band to play it.

By the time she reached "Judy, my Judy" in the second line, the audience was quiet. By the end of the song, they clamored for an encore. Ella complied by singing Pinky Tomlin's great song "The Object of My Affection." Chick Webb was in the audience and invited Ella to try out for his band.

Ella Fitzgerald was sixteen, a tall young woman with big shoulders and a rangy walk, who had never really dressed up to sing. Chick Webb wondered if she had stage presence and polish. But he knew she had the voice, and the audiences at the Savoy Ballroom loved her. She recorded "A-Tisket, A-Tasket" with lyrics she helped develop from her own childhood game, with the band in 1934. It became an enormous hit and made Ella an international star.

Chick Webb was a talented, tortured man who suffered from gradually more painful tuberculosis of the spine. By the time he died in 1939, at the age of only thirty-four, the band decided that its best ticket to continued success was to take the name of Ella and Her Famous Orchestra. But within three years, Ella struck out on her own.

Not only was she fascinated by bebop improvisations, she experimented with them herself, using her voice as Dizzy used his horn. Her scat singing technique was so complex, complete, and fluid, it was its own language. Listen to her revolutionary 1947 recording of the Gershwins' "Oh, Lady Be Good." The band essentially steps back to allow Ella to improvise chorus after chorus of brilliant, babbling, totally original music.

In the 1950s, Ella began a series of recordings that would move her from being a star to a legend. She recorded special selections of the music of George and Ira Gershwin, Irving Berlin, Rodgers and Hart, Cole Porter, Duke Ellington, Jerome Kern, and Johnny Mercer that Verve Records called "songbooks." "American Songbook" would become how the music we sang would be identified. And Ella Fitzgerald, who as a kid had had to escape from the mean streets, became the definitive interpreter of this sophisticated, complicated, intricate, and involving music that come to define a Golden Age of American music.

A great singer like Billie Holiday (and as soon as I see that in print, I need to add that no one was quite like Billie Holiday) sang so that you could feel the broken heart and slow tears in her voice. Ella, who had endured her own heartbreak and misery but didn't speak of it (or have to see it splashed all over the news), emphasized the exuberance of surviving, of staying alive, in her voice. Each of them made music out of hardship in her own way.

Ella recorded three albums with Louis Armstrong in the 1950s: *Ella and Louis, Ella and Louis Again,* and their own *Porgy and Bess.* There is no more purely joyful experience than to spend an evening binge-listening to all three, one after another, hearing these two giant talents being so playful as they romp through "Can't We Be Friends?," the Gershwins' "They Can't Take That Away from Me," Gus Kahn's "Makin' Whoopee," "Let's Call the Whole Thing Off," and a truly haunting version of "It Ain't Necessarily So" that opens gorgeously with Louis's horn, which essentially rolls out a sumptuous carpet for Ella to pick up the song in a way that both is stately—and swings. Their voices blended and mixed together like a great Old Fashioned.

I wound up living near Ella in Beverly Hills for a few years in the 1970s, though it seemed to me that we always ran into each other at airports. Ella famously worked forty-six weeks a year and was on the road for almost all of it. She was probably closest to her half sister, Frances, who died unexpectedly in 1966. Ella adopted Frances's three children—and then worked harder than ever to provide for them and put them through college. To be sure, she lived to work.

But Ella and I made a point of spending Christmas together almost every year that we were neighbors in the 1970s. Ella, who was alone by then, would come to the door and sweep my daughters, Antonia and Joanna, up in her arms. She'd say, "Oh, my daughters are finally here!" I can still smell the holiday dinner she'd have waiting for us.

In the contentious and back-biting enterprise of show business, Ella Fitzgerald was universally acclaimed and beloved. A man walking by her house in Beverly Hills was once bitten by her dog. He knocked on her front door, blood dripping from his ankle, all prepared to lecture the dog's owner and make dire threats about a lawsuit.

Then Ella opened the door.

"Oh," said the wounded man. "Ella Fitzgerald. Well, then, let's just forget about it"—and limped away.

Ella won thirteen Grammy Awards, a Kennedy Center Honor, and a whole lot more. But what I've taken from my memories of her so many times over the years was something she used to say to me when we talked about the troubles we had with various producers, business agents, or managers, or when we spoke about the struggles of the civil rights era.

As I look back on it now, it was probably something Ella learned from her early days on the streets of Harlem to keep body and soul alive. She used to fix her kind eyes on me, put her eloquent hands on my arm, and tell me, "Tony, just remember: we're all here."

Purple Flowers, Crystal

Pearl Bailey

In so many ways, I owe the life I've been blessed to enjoy in show business to the great Pearl Bailey. I was singing for a break, not a living, at the Village Inn in Greenwich Village. I'd show up at night and wait for an open spot on the bill, hoping that the owner would let me do a few songs for a free drink (and not top shelf, either). It was a good and honest way to try to get a break in the business; a lot of talented people never get even that break. But the longer you sing for free drinks, the more you begin to wonder if anyone is listening and where it will lead. You worry that you may never catch the break you've been working for.

The owner of the club decided that he'd try to update his entertainment policy. Singers and comics who worked for free drinks were affordable. But after a while, it's hard to attract people with a bunch of amateurs. He invited Pearl Bailey to come by and take a look at the club in the hope that she would consider playing there for a couple of weeks on a contract. Pearl was just coming off her first Broadway run in *St. Louis Woman*, a couple of movies, and her best-selling record *It Takes Two to Tango*.

I didn't know Pearl was in the audience that night. But when I got off, the owner told me, "Miss Bailey said, 'That Joe Bari guy stays on the bill. If you don't hire this boy, I'm not playing here.'" He smiled at me as he added, "And I was gonna tell you to take a hike."

Pearl headlined the club, and it changed my life. Her run got the attention of Bob Hope, which got him to the club, where he saw me and invited me to join him at the Paramount and then on tour. But it was, first and last, a nightly education to see the way Pearl Bailey put together a show and carried it from start to finish. She opened with a song with a moderate beat, as people got settled and sipped their drinks, then moved to a song with swing to bring them up in their seats, then a romantic number to draw them in, then a dramatic number to wrench their hearts. She was a total pro.

"I can give you a start, kid," she said to me once between shows. "But it will take you ten years to learn how to walk onstage." It took me ten years to figure out that Pearl meant it would take ten years of being a headliner to know how to take the stage and keep the audience with you for a whole show.

Pearl loved to mug for a friendly crowd and make them laugh with just a twitch of her hips, a quip, and a smile. She was a total entertainer. There was a girl in the chorus who began to imitate Pearl behind her back onstage, which drew a few laughs—and drew eyes from Pearl. The girl might have thought she was being clever. But she didn't understand the ethics of show business. Everyone onstage was trying to get ahead. But you support the star who's out there onstage, the way you back up a pilot in the cockpit. The star is the one who's out there, trying to land the show. You don't distract or mock her.

One night, Pearl caught the girl mimicking her out of the corner of her eye. In a flash, she turned around and slugged the girl. The dancer went down like a ton of bricks and stayed there. The audience roared. Pearl told them, "Well, folks, that's the end of the show. I can't top that," and they laughed and laughed. I guess they thought it was part of Pearl's act. In a way, it was. I wonder if the poor girl knew that Pearl hadn't slugged her because she was jealous (no one could outshine Pearl Bailey on a stage) but because the girl was undermining the job of everyone in the show.

Pearl was our star. She had the authority and even the responsibility to stop the dancer from clowning.

I suppose she could have just had a heart-to-heart conversation with the poor girl after the show. But Pearl put her message across eloquently, didn't she? The hell of it is, no one would have been a more loyal friend to the girl than Pearl Bailey, had the girl just been respectful. Pearl called herself my "Mama Pearl," and I bet she was that for quite a few other performers, too. If you treated Pearl with respect, she became your press rep, your sounding board, and your tireless advocate. Pearl never stopped looking for spots for me and talking me up to producers.

Pearl made a few high-profile films, including *Carmen Jones* in 1954 and *Porgy and Bess* in 1959. But it says a lot about racism in Hollywood in the 1950s and '60s that they couldn't find more roles for this ebullient, wise, magnetic performer. Pearl reminded the world of that when she broke records playing Dolly Levi in the all-African-American production of Jerry Herman and Michael Stewart's *Hello, Dolly!* That show broke the box

Japanese Garden, Tokyo

office on Broadway in 1967 and toured around the world for ten years. Pearl broke another record, too: for the most performances in the White House, even more than Bob Hope. She had a long, happy marriage to my friend Louis Bellson, the great drummer, and they adopted two great kids. Pearl received the Presidential Medal of Freedom from President Reagan in 1988.

Then, when she was nearly sixty, Pearl decided to get the college degree she had always longed to have since going to work in Philadelphia nightclubs at the age of fifteen. She enrolled in Georgetown University, which is no diploma mill, and gained a bachelor's degree in theology at the age of sixty-seven. I've sometimes wondered if the fine Jesuit scholars who were Pearl's professors at Georgetown had heard how she handled the girl behind her in the chorus line.

Over the years, I've often thought about another piece of advice Pearl gave me along the way. "Show business is a great life, Tony," she once said. "But you have to be careful about breathing the helium." She meant, of course, the way that inhaling applause and flattery can cloud your judgment when you need it most, especially offstage in real life.

I knew at the time that she was right. But sometimes we learn only by making our own mistakes. Over the course of my life, there were times I remembered what she told me and wished I'd taken her wisdom a little more to heart.

Still Life

Charlie Chaplin

I once stood in front of Charlie Chaplin's home on the banks of Lake Geneva in Switzerland for almost an hour, trying to work up the courage to knock on his door. We had never met. But we were not strangers.

Charlie had written the music for the theme and score of his extraordinary 1936 film *Modern Times*. John Turner and Geoffrey Parsons added lyrics to the tune in 1954, and it became the song we now know as "Smile."

I was lucky enough to record the song in 1959. Some of my fans consider it one of my best. I loved Charlie's smooth, swelling melody (he said it was inspired by Puccini's *Tosca*) and the lyrics that fit so beautifully:

Hide every trace of sadness
Although a tear may be ever so near . . .

A few months after the song climbed up the charts, I got a package from Switzerland. Charlie Chaplin had sent me the last ten minutes of *Modern Times*, in which he first used the song.

I was overwhelmed. There is no artist I have admired more than Charlie Chaplin. The breadth of his contributions is just staggering—as an actor, composer, director, producer, screenwriter—and a tramp, a clown, and a prince in what can be a demanding and seamy business.

I've read widely and deeply about Chaplin, searching through his life for clues about what sparked his genius.

Charlie had a childhood that could have been out of a Depression-era movie. His mother and father were music hall performers, his mother a chorine and his father a singer. But Charlie's father, Charles, Sr., left his family by the time Charlie was two and gave them no support. His mother, Hannah, had to scrounge for a living by taking on odd jobs, and Charlie and his brother, Sydney, who was four years older, were sent to the Central London District School for paupers. Charlie Chaplin was seven years old. Seven years old.

By the time Charlie was ten, Hannah had to go into a sanitarium. She had developed a mental illness that might have been aggravated by syphilis and certainly by malnutrition. Charlie and Sydney had outgrown the workhouse and were sent to live with their father. Charles, Sr., barely knew his sons and didn't care to know them. He was usually drunk and often cruel. He thrashed his sons. It is not really unkind to say that Charles, Sr., did his sons a service by dying at the age of thirty-eight from cirrhosis of the liver.

Sydney Chaplin had joined the Royal Navy at the age of fifteen, as soon as he could lie persuasively enough to convince the recruiters that he was old enough to enlist. He wanted to see the world, but mostly he wanted to get away. Charlie dropped out of school at the age of fourteen to try to care for his mother, who was in and out of the sanitarium. He often slept on the street and scrounged for food in alleys. But he had already begun to nurse dreams of a life in show business, and the manager of a theatrical agency in the West End must have seen something in the soiled, scruffy street kid who showed up at his office. I've sometimes wondered if I would have seen that spark, too.

Charlie got cast as a newsboy in a show that closed after two weeks. But he left enough of an impression that he was soon picked as a page boy in a production of *Sherlock Holmes* that wound up touring Great Britain and returning to the West End. The man who would become world famous as Charlie Chaplin had a role in a London hit by the time he was sixteen.

Sydney Chaplin (who would later become his brother's manager) had come out of the Royal Navy and began to tour in comedy sketches with his brother. It was Sydney Chaplin who was actually first signed for Fred Karno's prestigious music hall revue.

I think that Fred Karno's name is often a little overlooked in show business history. But early cinema, Charlie Chaplin, Hal Roach Studios, and Stan Laurel in particular were influenced by this great British comedy producer. Fred Karno may be the man who invented slapstick comedy, including cream pies in the face. Now, isn't that a contribution to culture?

Fred's broad, physical jokes reached the back of the house in the days before microphones. They were also a way of working around blue codes and censorship. How do you censor a performer who just pats his pants and rolls his eyes?

Sydney persuaded Karno to take on his younger brother for a couple of weeks. Fred was not enthusiastic. I've read that he thought young Charlie looked "pale, puny, and sullen-looking." But he could also see that he blossomed under the stage lights, and by the time Charlie was nineteen, he was playing the lead in Karno's sketch comedy revues.

Karno was preparing a troupe to tour North America. He made Charlie the headliner. Charlie blossomed under the new attention. He did a pantomime drunk act called "The Inebriate Swell," which drew rave reviews for his skilled physical comedy and use of silence, with his penguin walk, twitching lips, and swan dives onto the stage. It's hard for me not to think, though, that the sketch was also Charlie's way of turning his father's drunken flops and dives into a source of laughter, not misery. He turned painful memories into pratfalls.

The tour lasted twenty-one months and ranged all over the United States and Canada by train. By the time the Fred Karno troupe returned to the United Kingdom in the summer of 1912, neither Charlie, the United States, nor comedy would be the same. Charlie began a new US tour as soon as he could, in the fall of 1913.

Just a few months through his second American tour, Charlie was wooed to make pictures at Keystone Studios. Keystone wanted a new star. And Charlie, as he said, wanted a new life. I think that's why he got into show business in the first place. All of us who make a life onstage can understand that.

He began his career in a new medium with a mostly forgettable little 1914 film called *Kid Auto Races at Venice* (California, not Italy). Charlie plays a spectator at a kiddie auto race who keeps getting in the way of the race and fans. It's not a great movie when you see it now (if someone named Charlie Smith had made it, no one would be interested in it today) but a great experiment. Charlie unveiled the character that became known as "the Tramp," a sad sack of a soul in baggy pants, a too-small hat, and a stubby brush mustache that Charlie could twitch for laughs or droop for tears without concealing his expression.

His character looked, all at once, like no one else and Everyman.

"A tramp," Charlie said of his character, "a gentleman, a poet, a dreamer, a lonely fellow, always hopeful of romance and adventure."

Charlie Chaplin was one of the form's foremost creators. He built his own studios in southern California, where he produced, directed, and usually cowrote each film. He had not only what today we'd call total artistic control but total responsibility, which, as I learned the hard way, is even more difficult to acquire. Charlie was responsible for virtually every single aspect of his films, from the directions in a script to a burned-out bulb on his set. I think his films grew along with his artistic ambitions.

Charlie saw photographs of the Klondike Gold Rush from 1898 (it hadn't been a big story when he was growing up in London) and became fascinated with it. Then he heard about and began to explore the tragic tale of the Donner Party of 1847, frontier pioneers who'd had to resort to eating the deceased members of their party when they got trapped by heavy snow and food ran out. The film *The Gold Rush* that Charlie wrote, produced, starred in, and directed in 1925 was nothing less than a modern masterpiece, funny, touching, tragic, and romantic.

The Tramp (named the Lone Prospector for this film) gets lost in a blizzard while prospecting for gold and stumbles into the cabin of a criminal named Black Larsen. They are joined by a prospector named Big Jim. The three work out an uneasy truce in the cabin while they wait out the blizzard, but hunger soon stalks them. They cook one of the Prospector's shoes on Thanksgiving.

Charlie fishes the shoe from the stewpot, one bare foot revealed, and spools the shoelaces like spaghetti strings. He separates the sole from the upper leather as if deboning a fish, then takes a bite and makes a face, as if trying to figure out what wine would go best. I think the genius of that scene is that the men are so hungry that, in their minds, the Tramp makes the shoe taste like a dish at Maxim's de Paris. As

Charlie put it, "To truly laugh, you must be able to take your pain and play with it."

Charlie actually welcomed the addition of sound to movies. But not to make characters talk. I love that. He thought that nothing improved on pantomime to tell a story. But I think he welcomed the chance to use music, artfully added, to propel a story and give it feeling (besides, he thought the Tramp's Everyman quality would be diminished by his British accent, although every American character, from Superman to Hank Williams, is portrayed these days by a British actor).

By the time he made *Modern Times* in 1936, Chaplin knew how important the Tramp had become to millions of people. He made his character into a stand-in for Everyman on a factory assembly line, who is pressured to work harder and harder and faster and faster until he is made to feel like a cog in a vast machine and breaks down (and, rather like Charlie in real life, is mistaken for a Communist instigator); ultimately he finds love with a woman he helps and who helps him. Those last ten minutes of film that Charlie sent me are gorgeous and touching, with the Tramp and Ellen (beautifully played by Paulette Goddard), the hungry, resourceful girl he met after she stole a loaf of bread, finally walk into a sunrise and, we all hope, a new and better day.

It was his last film as the Tramp, by the way—until that signature moustache reappeared in 1940, with much more sinister tones, over the mouth of Adenoid Hynkel, the dictator of Tomainia, in *The Great Dictator*. Charlie and Adolf Hitler had been born just four days apart in 1889, both into poverty. I think Charlie had been struck by how one wanted to make the world laugh, the other to make the world bleed. Charlie had told his son, Charles, Jr., "He's the madman, I'm the comic. But it could have been the other way around."

Over the years, in all my reading about his life and studying his films and, in many ways, Charlie's life and creativity, what I've come to admire most about him was how he never stopped trying to undertake new and greater projects. He kept going forward as an artist, even as he became a controversial figure for his politics and his romantic life, which became the subject of seamy press coverage and even a couple of senseless trials.

"It takes courage to make a fool of yourself," he used to say.

By the time I stood outside his house, Charlie had been shut out of the United States, had sold his home in Beverly Hills and stake in United Artists, and was living with his wife Oona O'Neill Chaplin (Charlie was fifty-four and Oona eighteen when they met and married) in an estate overlooking Lake Geneva.

It must have been in the early 1960s. Charlie had been kind enough to send me the ten minutes of his film footage. But it was years before the Academy of Motion Picture Arts and Sciences would welcome him back to the United States to receive an Honorary Oscar in 1972.

I guess I wondered how he would receive an uninvited visitor from the United States. I guess I worried that he wouldn't recognize my name at first. I guess I felt that his privacy had already been picked apart by all the relentless publicity and I should just leave him alone. I guess that I just didn't want to disturb a great artist in his peace overlooking a splendid lake. So I just stared at his estate for a long time.

I'll always regret not knocking on Charlie Chaplin's door. I've met some of his friends and family members over the years who've said that he would have loved to meet me and my family. But I'll always have the great gift he gave me of his film, and the gift he gave all of us in an art form that he did so much to invent and elevate.

Gondola, Venice

Johnny Mercer

Johnny Mercer used to say that he wrote those heart-piercing lyrics for "One for My Baby (and One More for the Road)" on a napkin at the bar of P. J. Clarke's. "I'm feelin' so bad / Wish you'd make the music pretty and sad." A famous New York character named Tommy Joyce was the bartender there, and when the song became a hit, Johnny said he called him to apologize for writing, "So set 'em up, Joe."

"Sorry, Tommy," he said. "I tried but just couldn't get your name to rhyme."

(Try it yourself—Tommy is a tough one to rhyme.)

Johnny was born in Savannah, Georgia, to a prominent Georgia family that included Revolutionary War heroes and a Confederate general. His parents noticed that he loved music at an early age and took him to see minstrel shows and vaudeville troupes. But growing up in Savannah in the early twentieth century, Johnny heard the music that nourished jazz and the blues in the cries of street vendors and fishermen, singing in southern dialect. He was enthralled.

Johnny began to write songs, the kind of ditties and dog-gerels that kids will do, but with a jazz beat, when he went away to his southern prep school. He was supposed to go to Princeton—several generations of Mercers had—but his family was hard hit by the financial collapse of 1929.

So at the age of nineteen, he moved to New York. He did odd jobs by day and wrote and played music at night.

His first real break came in 1933, when he worked with the great song composer Hoagy Carmichael. Hoagy told interviewers that he was napping on the sofa in his New York studio when Johnny strolled in to begin their day at the piano.

"Hoag," he said Johnny told him, "I'm going to write a song called 'Lazy Bones.'" And then they did, in about twenty minutes.

Johnny said he'd always resented the "southern" songs New Yorkers wrote, which he found unreal and a little insulting. He and Hoagy wanted "Lazy Bones" to convey the swelter and tempo of the South in summer, so Johnny wrote:

Lazybones, sleepin' in the sun,
How you 'spect to get your day's work done?

The song was a huge hit just a few days after it was played on the radio. It was a southern song that had resonance in the North, East, West, and everywhere. What parent hasn't sung at least a few bars of "Lazy Bones" to try to get a child out of bed for school?

On the strength of that hit and a few more promising songs, Johnny moved out to Hollywood. It turned out to be the best thing for him. Movies were beginning to replace stage shows and revues, and close-mic recording techniques made lyrics more important than ever. Johnny's lyrics were clever, sly, and worth hearing.

Johnny won a reputation in Hollywood when he wrote both the music and the lyrics for "I'm an Old Cowhand (from the Rio Grande)," for a film called *Rhythm on the Range*. The film starred Bing Crosby and the great Frances Farmer. It was the only "western" Bing ever made, but he plays a citified rodeo cowboy who croons:

> *We know all the songs that the cowboys know*
> *'Bout the big corral where the doggies go*
> *We learned them all on the radio . . .*

It's still a wonderfully tuneful, witty and original song (although I've never recorded it—I'm not sure I could keep a straight face). *Rhythm on the Range* practically invented the "singing cowboy" genre. In fact, watch the song in the film: you'll see the young Roy Rogers, singing behind Bing and Frances in the chorus, and Louis Prima, who was an even more improbable cowpoke than Bing, playing the trumpet.

Johnny began to write great songs with Richard Whiting, including "Too Marvelous for Words" and the fabulous standard "Hooray for Hollywood" (a song with twenty true quotable lines, including "Hooray for Hollywood / Where you're terrific if you're even good"). After Richard died, too young, Johnny worked with the great Harry Warren and got his first Oscar nomination in 1938 for "Jeepers Creepers." They would go on to win the Academy Award for Best Original Song with "On the Atchison, Topeka, and the Santa Fe" in 1946.

Soon thereafter, Johnny began to work with the elegant Harold Arlen. Their songs began to set a new standard, including "Blues in the Night" and "One for My Baby" in 1941 and "Come Rain or Come Shine" in 1946. Their music was distinguished by a wise, sultry quality. They were songs for the long nights of the soul. Who hasn't had those?

The rise of rock and roll threw us all a bit. But Johnny kept working and came roaring back, winning consecutive Oscars for two of the greatest movie songs ever. He wrote the lyrics for Henry Mancini's "Moon River" from *Breakfast at Tiffany's* in 1961, and then returned the very next year to win for "Days of Wine and Roses."

I'm so grateful that around that time, Johnny got a note from a fan named Sadie Vimmerstedt in Youngstown, Ohio, who told him she thought that "I want to be around to pick up the pieces when somebody breaks your heart . . ." would make great first lines for a song. Johnny thought so, too. "I Wanna Be Around" became one of my biggest hits. Sadie gave Johnny a great beginning. But only Johnny Mercer could write a line like "When he breaks your heart to bits / Let's see if the puzzle fits so fine."

What I think I appreciated most and learned from Johnny is the way he wrote great songs with so many gifted composers over the years. His partnership with Harold Arlen was something special and extraordinary. But he also had superb working partnerships with amazing, singular talents, including Hoagy Carmichael, Richard Whiting, Harry Warren, Henry Mancini—and Sadie Vimmerstedt, for that matter. And other composers, too.

In each case, he drew strength from his collaborators and learned something new each time he worked with them. He learned from everyone and from every project. If you're going to make a life in arts and entertainment, that helps keep you going. It helps keep you fresh.

In 1939, Johnny wrote the lyrics to a song by Ziggy Elman. Ziggy (his parents didn't name him that; he was born Harry Finkelman in Philadelphia) was a great trumpeter who had his own orchestra for a while but was probably best known for playing with Benny Goodman. Ziggy wrote a short song as an instrumental he worked into his show. Johnny heard the tune and was inspired to write those touching, universal lines that include one of the greatest, simplest professions of love ever: "You smile, and the angels sing." Naturally, those last four words became the title of the song.

Ziggy never wrote another hit. He wound up, according to reports, going bankrupt and working in a music store. But the song he wrote became a number one hit in America.

Johnny died in 1976. He's buried in Hollywood, and his tombstone reads, "And the Angels Sing." They do. And Johnny heard their voices, took it all down, and gave me those great songs to sing.

Philippine Islands, Manila

Louis Prima

I always called Louis Prima a wild man onstage. But I never met a shrewder showman.

"The Chief," as he was known, played the trumpet beautifully, sang distinctively, built bands, and pranced and swayed onstage in total control of his show from beginning to end. He was a total showman.

Louis grew up in an Italian neighborhood of New Orleans, where gambling was open and overlooked, if not exactly legal. But in his shrewd mind, he always took notes. When Las Vegas began to develop, he knew more about gambling than the operators who took out licenses. He told them where to put the showrooms and the gambling floors, and how to run the house and make it pay. I think Louis Prima was as important to the success of show business in Las Vegas as the railroad and Hoover Dam.

Louis played the violin at his church parish when he was a boy, but he soon followed the trail of jazz when he heard some of the African American masters, including Louis Armstrong. He was playing in French Quarter clubs by the time he finished high school. Then he took a chance, went to New York for Mardi Gras season, and got his first gigs playing at the famous Shim Sham Club, where he met Guy Lombardo.

Louis said that because he was from New Orleans, played jazz, worshipped Louis Armstrong, sang scat, and had a swarthy complexion and curly hair from his Sicilian family, there were club owners who thought he was black. He was sure he lost out on jobs because of that.

But then World War II came, and Louis was declared 4-F. He got a lot of gigs, and those jobs really helped his career take off. Despite the fact that Italy was at war with the United States, Louis's biggest hits were Italian songs (or at least what sounded Italian to a lot of Americans), including "Felicia No Capicia," "Bacci Galupe (Made Love on the Stoop)," "Please No Squeeza Da Banana," and "Angelina," which happened to be the name of Louis's mother. You couldn't really get away with singing lyrics like "I eat zoop-ing minestrone / Just to be with her alone / Angelina," today, but in the 1940s, Louis made those songs a laughing, winking tribute to the way millions of Italian American families had become so much a part of the United States that they could kid themselves and openly retain their love for an Italy that was unsoiled by Il Duce.

I expressed pride in my Italian heritage with what's often called bel canto singing, where words and even pauses are stressed to emphasize emotional content. But Louis was a great, sentimental Pagliacci clown of a singer, who did it his own way.

Louis Prima opened for me a lot of times over the years. We enjoyed working together, Louis with his broad comedy and antics and Old World songs, me singing contemporary ballads and love songs. It was a winning combo, especially in the years when Louis was married to and performed with the fabulous Keely Smith.

I also knew that Louis's matchless zing always got an audience going. Lots of performers over the years have told me to never open my act with a performer of equal stature. But I've always counted myself blessed to have the likes of Duke Ellington, Count Basie, Lena Horne, and Louis Prima open for me. They always raised the temperature in the room—for me, too. They didn't make me despair to come out when they were done but inspired me to do my best.

Louis also gave me a wise bit of advice that, by the time I felt free to ignore it, I think he would have agreed to, too. He told me, "Always get top billing, Tony. Work a smaller room, if you want to, even a sawdust joint, but always be the headliner."

I'm sure he wasn't wrong. But by the time those opportunities came along, it was when I was asked to work with Duke Ellington, Count Basie, and Frank Sinatra. Being asked to share the stage with them was such an honor, it seemed crazy and inconsiderate to spend even a second wrangling over which name went first or in larger letters. I was just grateful for the chance to have my name alongside theirs in any combination.

Besides, Louis didn't always follow his own good advice. He agreed to be the voice of King Louis, an orangutan, who appears in Walt Disney's animated 1967 film of Rudyard Kipling's *Jungle Book* (Louis's character does not appear in the Kipling version, so don't even look for it).

Historical accounts say that Walt Disney had initially wanted Louis Armstrong to voice the role. But he had to retract the offer to avoid criticism of casting a great black musician to be the voice of an orangutan—so they asked another New Orleans musician, who was Sicilian American, to play a singing monkey. I guess that was considered progress in 1967.

Louis was cast alongside other great personalities with distinctive voices, including Phil Harris as a sloth, Sebastian Cabot as a snooty black panther, and George Sanders as a cold-blooded Bengal tiger. Louis got to sing a great Sherman brothers song, "I Wanna Be Like You," and became famous among a whole new generation of fans, and for generations to come, whenever the movie is downloaded for kids. Even as the cartoon that he voiced, Louis Prima was the complete showman. He reminded me that this is what entertainment is all about.

Central Park Skyline

"London By Night"   Benedetto '84

London by Night

Amy Winehouse

I met Amy Winehouse in 2008 without really meeting her. I presented the Record of the Year Grammy Award to Amy for her well-regarded hit song "Rehab." But she couldn't be there to accept it. She had been in rehab in London, and the US Embassy there had refused to give her a visa. The State Department ultimately relented, but too late for Amy to fly to Los Angeles for the ceremony.

So all I saw after I announced her name was a beautiful, sloe-eyed young woman on the television monitor, her dark hair piled high, her long, pale arms richly tattooed, who gasped, laughed, cried, then jumped into the arms of her Island Records colleagues and her parents.

I liked that. "This is for all of you," she said. "And this is for London!"

By the way: Amy Winehouse won five Grammy Awards that night, tying the record for a night's haul. But she told the press her biggest thrill was to hear a singer who had been important to her say her name. Of course, the honor was mine.

I loved Amy's spirit as soon as I saw her, shocked, humbled, then exhilarated. I already loved her truly great voice, which was powerful, expressive, and affecting.

We met again three years later, at the famous Abbey Road Studios, to record that great Johnny Green song "Body and Soul," for my *Duets II* CD. She didn't have to be told about the history of the song, which had originally been written for Gertrude Lawrence. But over the years, it's become perhaps the most recognizable jazz standard ever, recorded by Billie Holiday, Etta James, Sarah Vaughan, and Frank Sinatra and in instrumental versions by John Coltrane, Bill Evans, Charlie Mingus, Thelonious Monk, and an especially influential rendition in 1939 by Coleman Hawkins.

Amy was of a much younger generation. But she'd grown up in London in a family of jazz lovers. Her favorite singer as a kid hadn't been Madonna or Cher, worthy as they are, but Dinah Washington. Amy's father used to sing Sinatra songs to her. She said that whenever she was called into the principal's office, she would sing "Fly Me to the Moon" to herself to lift her spirits.

Amy Winehouse was a star by the time she was twenty. Her first album, *Frank* (the title partly a signal that the songs were drawn from her own life and feelings and partly a sly salute to Frank Sinatra), went platinum and was nominated for BRIT Awards. Over the next few years, she worked to perfect a singular style that paid homage to soul, girl-group pop, and jazz but became instantly recognizable as her own. She fretted over all aspects of production, from the song to the recording to getting it into stores. Her father, Mitch, drove a London cab. He recalled how Amy would come out of a studio with a recording to play in his taxi, just to test how it would sound to a passenger who was riding in a car.

She quickly became famous in the United States and around

the world. But as her fame grew, so did stories that seemed to show that she was having a hard time handling the heady combination that talent and fame can bring. And she was already too famous to make her mistakes in private.

The more successful she became, the more pressure she felt to succeed. The more money she made, the more she had to make to fuel her expanding musical enterprise. The pressure to succeed is hard enough for young people to bear. But the pressure to keep producing hits can make you anxious, sleepless, and scared, which can lead you to look for comfort and relief in all the wrong places, often beginning with alcohol and drugs.

The British press would be filled with stories about Amy failing to show for concerts or showing up hours late, slurring the words to her songs and stumbling. She was booed off the stage more than once, even as her music sold millions. A few times she had to cancel appearances for days or weeks to rest and seek help.

But that wasn't the Amy Winehouse I met that day at Abbey Road Studios. Amy was engaging, funny, charming, and utterly professional but a little bit shy.

She met Danny Bennett, my son the producer. Then Daegal Bennett, our engineer, came in to adjust her microphone.

"My son," I told Amy.

"Is everyone here your son?" she asked. "How many kids do you have here?"

But she was noticeably nervous. She said she was nervous because she had never recorded a song with someone she considered to be one of her idols. After running through a few bars of the song, she said that she hadn't recorded for a long time—her only reference to the problems she'd been living through.

We went through a couple of takes, just to feel our way into the song. We each had a couple of stumbles, and Amy was hard on herself.

"I don't want to waste your time," she said. I assured Amy that she wasn't; and besides, we had all day.

When I told her that her voice reminded me of Dinah Washington's, Amy began to gush and tell me how devoted she had been to Dinah. I told her a few of my favorite Dinah Washington stories (how Dinah would come to Las Vegas with no advance bookings, just put down her two suitcases, knowing that some smart club owner would make room for her and the town would flock to see her). Each time we ran through "Body and Soul," I could see Amy making the changes of a great jazz artist, trying, testing, perfecting. Taking chances—and always different chances. It was thrilling to stand alongside her and share the journey through making a great song sound utterly fresh and distinctive.

She had the voice of an angel: a being that works on a plane higher than the one most of us inhabit down here.

The recording of "Body and Soul" that Amy Winehouse and I completed that day is one of the favorites of my career, and certainly one of my most praised and best selling. Amy put just the right touch of longing, the feeling of being both captivated and a little trapped by love and desire, into each phrase.

But by the time our recording was released on September 14, 2011, Amy's birthday, she had already left us. She died of alcohol poisoning on July 23. She was twenty-seven years old.

I was on the road, and Danny called me. I began to weep. For Amy. For her family and fans. And with a head full of questions and regrets for myself.

Should I have said something to Amy about the drugs and drinking? Should I have told her that I'd contended a little bit with that myself and knew how you can fall into a bad cycle, but I also knew that you could bring yourself back? Would it have made a difference if someone she considered an idol had said to her something like, "You're my idol. You are a once-in-a-lifetime talent. Please don't take that from the world." Or should I have said, "Walk away from it all, if you like. Just live. Please."

I've known enough people (including myself) who've contended with addiction to know that there's no "silver bullet" of a sentence you can say that will always help. But that doesn't mean you should always say nothing. Sometimes—sometimes—someone will say something that strikes home on just the right day. I said nothing on the day that I might have had a chance.

Our "Body and Soul" received the Grammy for Best Pop Duo/Group Performance the following February. Mitch Winehouse accepted Amy's award with his wife, Janis, and said, "We shouldn't be here. Our darling daughter should be here. These are the cards that we're dealt."

To this day, the proceeds from the sale of our single benefit the Amy Winehouse Foundation, which supports organizations that try to help young people with addiction problems. And as I reached my ninetieth birthday, I wished Amy were here so we could sing together again at all the celebrations.

Adele, Duffy, and Paloma Faith, other great British singers, have cited Amy as a real force in clearing the way on the pop charts for women who have roots in jazz and sing music that can't be pinned down into a genre. So have Lana Del Rey, my friend Lady Gaga, and the vocalist Sam Smith. Amy Winehouse took chances for them all. She took the spirit of jazz and made it shine in new ways, for a new generation. And Amy's memory reminds me how the music we bring to our lives goes on and on in those we love.

Burano, Italy

Ralph Sharon

Ralph Sharon played just a few notes for me, and I knew
we could make beautiful music together.

It was 1957, and I needed a new piano player. We held
auditions at the Nola Rehearsal Studio in midtown Manhattan.
As I remember it, Ralph was the second guy, and we didn't have
to go any further. He introduced himself, and I caught his British accent. Ralph told me he'd played with Ted Heath and His
Music, the leading British jazz band, from the time he was in his
late teens (though I wouldn't learn for a few months that *Down
Beat* magazine of England had declared him to be the Best Jazz
Pianist in Britain) and had come to the United States about four
years before.

"I grew up in the Tube during the Blitz," he said. "I wanted
to go somewhere I could see sunlight."

Ralph was a tall man, beginning to bald then, with a mild
smile and exquisite manners. He'd played with Carmen McRae
and Johnny Hartman in the United States and said that his

heart was in jazz. Then he turned around on the bench, spread his long fingers across the keys, and began to play.

I was entranced by his touch and delicacy. Within a few seconds, I knew he was the man I wanted to accompany me for all my songs, in studios and on the road.

"How'd you like to come with me?" I asked him.

"Come with you where?" asked Ralph.

"Everywhere," I told him.

Within a few weeks, Ralph and I were in our first recording session together. Ralph loved jazz, sensed my love of jazz, and helped put the steel in my spine to stand up for the kind of music I believed in and to sing and record it.

"You can have six hits in a row," he told me, "but if you keep doing the same thing over and over, the public will get bored and stop buying your records. If you keep singing these kinds of sweet saccharine songs like 'Blue Velvet,' sooner or later the ax is going to drop on you."

So Ralph and I came up with what amounted to a formula: we'd do one record for Columbia, then one for us.

Ralph and I laid out a plan to record "The Beat of My Heart" later that year, which featured the great jazz drummers Art Blakey and Chico Hamilton, Nat Adderly on trumpet, and Herbie Mann on jazz flute. We did inventive new versions of "Just One of Those Things," in which I sang most of the song accompanied just by Art's superb drum work, and "Lullaby of Broadway."

Ralph conducted all of those superb musicians, too, and though we didn't sell as many records as "In the Middle of an Island," "The Beat of My Heart" is now considered a classic. It signaled that I wasn't just another crooner but a singer who loved jazz and wanted to bring its many gifts of artistry and improvisation into the music I loved. The collaborations with Count Basie, Duke Ellington, and other great names all followed.

None of that would have been possible without Ralph Sharon along. As he used to say, "I was the missing ingredient."

Ralph was a great piano player, who would record dozens of albums on his own. But I especially treasured that he was a superb—even the perfect—accompanist. He didn't play a melody and just expect a singer to follow. We always performed a subtle, unspoken duet, in which Ralph knew when to pull back, when to go ahead, and how to strike a note just right alongside my voice. We got better and more practiced at that over fifty years of working together, sometimes three hundred shows a year. But to be sure, we felt a lot of closeness from the first.

And of course, Ralph had the wisdom and talent to find the sheet music to "I Left My Heart in San Francisco" one night in a shirt drawer in the dresser of his hotel room in Hot Springs, Arkansas, a story told earlier in this book. That song took us around the world, in so many ways. But he always said, "If I hadn't looked for that shirt in that drawer, it would never have happened."

I'd only add, yes, but Ralph made sure it was in the drawer. What did Branch Rickey say? "Luck is the residue of design."

Ralph left my side, amicably, for a few years in the mid-sixties. He still craved sunshine and wanted to live on the West Coast. He also wanted to spend more time with his family. I was lucky enough to be able to ask Torrie Zito to be my accompanist. Torrie had worked with so many great names, including Frank Sinatra, Billie Holiday, and Billy Eckstine (and would go on to arrange the strings for John Lennon's classic 1971 *Imagine* album). It was like getting DiMaggio to step in for Gehrig in the lineup.

Ralph did superb work with Rosie Clooney, Nancy Wilson, Robert Goulet, and many more, and liked to stay home more than he had in years. His son, Bo, liked to recall that when he finished a gig at the Hollywood Bowl or some other glamorous venue, where big stars would come backstage and want to meet him, Ralph would just say to his family, "C'mon, let's get dinner and go home." Nothing was more important to Ralph than his family, his wife, Linda, and his son, Bo.

But I was so pleased when Danny Bennett, my son, essentially took over my career years later and asked Ralph to come along, too. It was at least the second time Ralph took a chance on me. My career had hit some deep skids in the 1970s, and Danny told me that I would come back only if I was willing to stop making compromises, sing what I loved, and let young audiences see that I was authentic and uncompromising. It reminded me of what Ralph had said. Once again, he rode shotgun for me.

I suppose that over fifty years of performing together, there is no one I have thanked more than Ralph Sharon. He deserves even more. He won scores of awards: Grammy Awards; the British Academy of Songwriters, Composers and Authors Gold Badge of Merit; and so many more. But he barely seemed to notice the honors that piled up, and he played into his nineties.

In 2001, years after he had "retired" to Boulder, Colorado, when he was almost eighty, he still played gigs, including at teatime at the fabulous old St. Julien Hotel. Sometimes jazz lovers would see his name on a card in the hotel and say, "You know, you have the same name as a really famous pianist." Ralph would just smile and say something like, "So I hear."

I'm still inspired and guided by what Ralph told me so many years ago, in so many words: keep growing, and believe in what you do. I lost a real brother when Ralph passed away in 2015. I hope to keep going for a while. But it's nice to know that when my time comes, Ralph and I will accompany each other.

Rio de Janeiro

New York Still Life

40

Lady Gaga

O ur partnership caused a lot of raised eyebrows when we first got together. What could Tony Bennett, a guy who was always turned out in a suit and tie and often a tux, have in common with the woman who wore a meat dress (raw flank steak, specifically) to the 2010 MTV Video Music Awards?

Well from the first, Stefani Joanne Angelina Germanotta and I discovered that we actually have a lot in common. We love and respect the music we sing—and each other.

We both appeared at a gala in May 2011 for the Robin Hood Foundation, a fine group that works to fight poverty in the New York metro area. I knew who Lady Gaga was; my son and manager, Danny Bennett, had made sure that I saw her HBO special in performance at Madison Square Garden.

In that show Gaga sang an especially dazzling version of "Born This Way," the number one single that she wrote with Jeppe Laursen, which has become a kind of anthem for many young gays ("Don't be a drag," she sings, "just be a queen . . . "). At one point, Gaga dropped all the thumping percussion and electric synth sounds and just sang a cappella (remember, I do that with at least one song in all of my shows, too). It was gorgeous and gutsy, strong and soaring.

I saw Gaga's superlative stagecraft, flash, and pyrotechnics. But I also heard a superb vocal artist at work who combined great musical skill with a depth of human feeling.

The night of the gala, Gaga sang "Orange Colored Sky," a great Nat "King" Cole song written by Milton DeLugg and Willie Stein. I love that song. I admired Gaga's taste in choosing a song that her fans might not know and expect, and I appreciated the style and artistry she brought to it.

I went backstage to meet her. Gaga was there with her parents, who seemed delighted that I had enjoyed their daughter's performance so much. It was one of the first things I liked about Lady Gaga: of all the people that the hottest singer in show business could bring to the MTV awards, she had brought her parents.

With no preamble and not much more than a handshake I said to Gaga, "Let's do an album together." She said, "Okay." My son Danny is a great producer, so his idea of getting me and Lady Gaga together for an album was brilliant. Within just a few days, Lady Gaga and I were in the music business together.

Gaga told me that jazz had been the first music she loved, growing up in an Italian family on the Upper West Side. She loved Billie Holiday in particular, especially the way she seemed to put all she had been through and all that she felt into the dusky shadings of her voice.

"You can tell that she's really been through something," Gaga once said. "I find that to be more exciting and interesting."

But her favorite was probably Ella Fitzgerald, for her total mastery and ability to improvise.

Of course, Ella and Billie were a couple of my favorites, too.

Gaga grew up listening to music that her father loved (so did I), and most of that music was classic jazz and blues. (And her father's rock albums. In fact, Gaga's name came from "Radio Ga Ga," Freddie Mercury's 1984 song with Queen.)

Lady Gaga's parents were Manhattan Internet entrepreneurs. They had more means than my family in Astoria, Queens, had had. But both Gaga's mother and father were hard workers who put fourteen hours a day into supporting their family, just as my parents worked long hours in a grocery store and a dress factory to support ours.

Gaga started performing when she was a kid, at about the same age as I was when I sang when Mayor La Guardia opened the Triborough Bridge.

Gaga went to NYU's Tisch School of the Arts and studied art and design, as well as music. I studied painting and music at New York's School of Industrial Arts before World War II began and went to the American Theatre Wing school when I came home from the army.

I worked as a singing waiter. Gaga was a waitress and coat-check girl. We both know what it's like to work hard, study hard, put your life and dreams out there, and take a chance. We've both tried to steer our performing lives by the advice that Mimi Speer, my old teacher at the American Theater Wing school, once gave me: "Don't imitate another singer. You'll just become a member of the chorus if you do."

And of course no one is like Lady Gaga.

We began our musical association by recording "The Lady Is a Tramp," the great Rodgers and Hart song we both love, at

Abbey Road Studios in London. One of the first things you see about Gaga when you work together in the studio is her utter professionalism and thoughtfulness. She doesn't just sweep in, like some other stars, oblivious to others. She stops to shake hands and talk to the engineers, the musicians, the office personnel, and the people who run out for bagels and coffee. She is that rare, huge talent who knows that you need to nurture and encourage collaboration to become a truly big star.

Gaga and I got better together as we went along. But from the first, there were sparks, banter, and a kind of effortless back-and-forth that inspired improvisation. It was fun, and it was electric.

We followed our single in 2014 with an ambitious project, *Cheek to Cheek*, an album rooted in jazz. It included the title track, Irving Berlin's song, Cole Porter's "Anything Goes," Duke's "It Don't Mean a Thing," and a haunting solo by Gaga of Billy Strayhorn's "Lush Life."

Lady Gaga told me she had first sung "Lush Life" when she was thirteen, with the Regis High School boys' choir. Billy's song came out of his own boredom and doubts about nightlife in "come what may places" after a lost romance. It is a beautifully intricate, emotionally nuanced song about love, loss, and the holes in your heart that never quite heal.

Nat "King" Cole and Billy Eckstine did the classic versions, I think. Sarah Vaughan, Blossom Dearie, Chet Baker, and Linda Ronstadt have done great ones, too. Gaga's belongs at the top of that select chart.

"I didn't know what the song was about when I first sang it," she once said. "Now I know *everything* that song is about."

At the time we recorded that song, Lady Gaga had already enjoyed enormous success. She had also discovered how that often comes with a lot of self-doubts and questions. There were people who pretended to be her friends but mostly wanted to attach themselves to her trajectory into the stars—and her money.

Gaga sang "Lush Life" beautifully and truly. Then she came into the control room and wept. I know that feeling. She had felt the song in the center of her soul and put all that she is and who she is into each line until she had given everything.

"Am I a mess, Tony?" she asked me over and over. "You are not a mess," I kept telling her. "You are a sophisticated lady."

Cheek to Cheek, by the way, debuted at the top of the *Billboard* 200 when it rolled out. It made Gaga the first woman artist of the decade to have three number one albums and me the oldest artist ever to hold the number one spot.

There is no mistaking the fact that the collaboration I've enjoyed with Lady Gaga has made me and the music to which I've devoted my artistic life appreciated by a whole new generation. They have kept me going past the age of ninety. And they have kept the music going on and on and on, into new generations.

But her friendship has also helped me make new discoveries in old songs and brought a fresh dimension to me in all ways. When we began to work together, I told her, "Just be yourself." And as so often happens, you realize that the advice you give someone else is really meant for yourself. Gaga helped me appreciate the artistic choices I've made in my career: Strive for quality. Don't settle for what's cheap and easy. Don't go for the number one hit—build a whole career.

We've toured all over the world together, and I always learn something new from the discoveries she makes in songs that by now we've done over and over. I sometimes look across the stage as we sing that lovely Jimmy Van Heusen song "But Beautiful" and think when we get to the lines "Beautiful to take a chance / And if you fall you fall," that Lady Gaga lives that with each and every song she sings.

I was so touched at my ninetieth birthday party on August 3, 2016, when Gaga sang "Orange Colored Sky" to mark our first meeting, and then "I Left My Heart in San Francisco"—my signature song, but in her signature way.

We were being interviewed once, and I heard Gaga say that one of the things she's learned from our partnership is that "You don't have to fear growing older. In my generation, this is like at the center of everything, especially in celebrity culture: it's all about staying young and staying perfect and staying youthful. . . . But Tony has remained the same, and there's nothing hipper. There's nothing hipper than being talented at something that you love, in having passion, and that is classic, and that is timeless."

Did you catch that? I think Lady Gaga called me hip.

Central Park, New York

Still Life, Crow Landing

41

Susan Benedetto

H ow did you two meet?" is an intriguing question people ask my beloved wife, Susan Benedetto, and me.
Let me just begin the story this way: the first time we
met, we didn't really see each other. Let me explain. . . .

It was 1966. Susan's parents, Marion and Dayl Crow, were
visiting New York from the San Francisco area, where they were
from. In fact, Marion Crow's family have been San Franciscans
since the mid-1800s. They were dedicated fans. I learned later
on that they had seen many of my shows.

Marion and Dayl came to see me perform at the Copacabana,
and in those days the cigarette girls would come around to all
the guests that wanted to have a photo taken at the table. Marion jokingly said, "Only if Tony Bennett is in the photo, too!"
To the Crows' surprise, after the show the cigarette girl, who
had gotten a note to me backstage, escorted them back to my
dressing room. I took the photo with them. As fate would have
it, Marion was pregnant at the time with . . . Susan! It's a photo

we all laugh about, knowing the incredible turn of events that followed.

Through her parents, Susan was introduced to my music and actually was the president of my fan club in the Bay Area as a teenager. When she was nineteen, she had tickets to see me perform at the Masonic Temple in San Francisco, and she put in a request to say hello backstage after the show, probably not even expecting a response. The request was sent to me, and it tickled me that someone of her age was so devoted to my music. I not only agreed to say hello to her backstage but asked her to be my date for the evening, and that's how it all really began, foreshadowed by a backstage photo taken in 1966!

I can't say that we didn't notice the age difference when we first met.

But I can say that after all these years together, we don't notice it much now. We're compatible in all ways. We appreciate the same music; we love films, especially old classics (and sometimes old B pictures that are hardly classics but have interesting twists or notable character actors); art; painting; and literature. Susan is a woman with a wise, mature character.

Susan came east and got her BA in history at Fordham, then went on to spend a year on an internship at the Reagan White House before getting her master's degree at Columbia University's Teachers College.

It was so appropriate for Susan to go into teaching, as it reflected her kind, caring, and intelligent disposition. She began her teaching career and then got her master's degree in supervision and administration from Fordham.

I've learned that Susan is thoughtful, and always truthful. She's brought balance and contentment into my life. Her goodness and the peace at the center of her soul have helped me to think straight, live well, and, I'm quite sure, live longer.

Susan is with me when I travel to perform, all over the world, and we share the discovery of new and old places. She has made our life into a journey that we share.

It is a journey that Susan and I also began to support arts education. This started when I attended Frank Sinatra's funeral in May 1998 (on Frank's gravestone it's chiseled, THE BEST IS YET TO COME), and I had in my mind to do something to honor his passing. Years ago, Rosemary Clooney and I had talked to Goddard Lieberson, who was then head of Columbia Records, about starting an arts school to allow students to explore all of the creative arts with encouragement and support.

That idea never got off the ground back then. But it stuck with me. Those two thoughts—honoring Frank and creating an arts school—came together, and I spoke to Susan about it when I returned from Frank's funeral. We both thought, Well, why not?

Susan, who was teaching at Fiorello H. La Guardia High School of Music & Art and Performing Arts in New York City, got to work. We consulted with many colleagues and educators, but it was my good friend Peter Vallone, whose family in Astoria gave me some of my earliest breaks in show business, who really pushed things along. At the time, Peter was head of the New York City Council, so with him on board we were able to meet with the mayor's team and the New York City Board of Education at City Hall. After attending many planning meetings, Susan and I were able to put our dream into reality. In fact, I vividly remember that Peter Vallone and I were standing on the steps of the Metropolitan Museum of Art, where we were holding my seventy-fifth birthday party, when he told me that the school had been approved.

From that point, Susan and I dedicated ourselves to creating a public arts high school that would provide the best arts education, along with a strong academic program. But we also wanted to nurture good citizens by having the students give back to their community and get involved with local organizations to perform and exhibit their artistic talents to enrich the community. I love the borough of Queens, where I grew up, so in 2001, we were able to open temporary quarters for a school for 250 students. And, true to my original intention, we named it Frank Sinatra School of the Arts.

The school flourished at its temporary site, but while that was going on, Susan and I gathered all our friends and colleagues to raise funds for the permanent site, which we wanted to be in Astoria. My hometown had given me so much when I started out that it was important to me to be able to give back to it. After years of hard work, and the generosity of many friends and donors and partners, including the American Ballet Theatre, Tribeca Film Institute, Museum of Modern Art, Juilliard, and many other partners, we opened our splendid new headquarters for Frank Sinatra School of the Arts in Astoria, Queens, in 2009. It's part of the Kaufman Astoria Studios complex, and we owe a debt of gratitude for all time to George Kaufman, who donated the land on which the school was built.

It's a school, and it's also a gathering place and cultural spot for the community. The building has an eight-hundred-seat concert hall, where I've been able to introduce my friends Lady Gaga, Billy Joel, Paul McCartney, Alec Baldwin, and many more to perform, and have had incredible speakers such as the late Governor Mario Cuomo, Harry Belafonte, Jerry Seinfeld, Wynton Marsalis share their wisdom with the students. Black box theaters, a stagecraft workshop, art studios and a gallery, dance studios, orchestral classrooms, recording booths, and an outdoor rooftop performance garden are some of the attributes that the school provides its students, and we are so proud of all that the students have been able to accomplish over the years.

It's a school, yes, for kids who are sure that they want to be artists. But it's also a school with top-rate academics for kids who may decide to go on to be engineers, scientists, IT professionals, business owners, and self-starters of all kinds. The arts will stay with them and make them better and deeper human beings. And when we saw the impact that this one school had on so many young people, Susan and I decided not to stop. As of this writing, through our nonprofit organization, Exploring the Arts, we partner with thirty-three public arts high schools in New York City and Los Angeles and have plans to expand further.

Susan has that effect on all of us. She is the greatest partner of all—in the school we founded and in my life.

Funny, I'm a guy who has sung some of the world's great love songs for decades and decades. But knowing Susan has revealed the beating heart of love to me. Susan Benedetto has shown me how love gives you the confidence and courage to be your best self, and the inner peace and contentment that come with them. This wonderful woman has made me a better man.

Cipriani, Venice

42

Giovanni "John" Benedetto

I suppose that every son thinks that his father is one of the strongest men he's known. But I'm sure that it's true of John Benedetto. My father died when I was just ten. Yet I still have vivid memories of his strong arms holding me close. I'd be rocked in his arms and stare into his deep, dark eyes until I fell asleep, knowing that those strong arms and that wise man would protect me in this world. I still feel that way.

My father was sick for just about all his life. He probably had rheumatic fever as a child, which would have damaged his heart. But there were no doctors, as we would use the term today, in Calabria in 1895, when my father was born, and no hospitals. People went to the old folks of the village if they were sick. Their "diagnosis" was often some kind of folktale and the prescription some kind of folk cure.

Like a lot of children who have health problems, my father learned early how to keep himself amused and interested. I know that he loved music and would often hike up to the tops of mountains in Calabria and sing, hearing his voice fill the valley. It must have made a sick little boy know that really he was very strong, in all of the important ways.

I am sure that my love of music runs back through my father. He sang for everyone—our family, our friends, and strangers who passed by our house. He had a lovely voice and would sit on the stairs in Astoria and sing opera, show music, and current pop hits to my brother and me in a fine, clear voice. I like to think that you can still hear my father's voice in me. I know I do.

My father was thoughtful, sensible, and sensitive. He was the man whom everyone in our family, and even in our neighborhood, sought out for advice, I think because he would listen, treat the other person with respect, and try to reply with sympathy, even if he or she didn't always take the advice he gave.

People didn't see psychiatrists in those days, and they didn't want to be seen seeking out the advice of a priest. So they went to John Benedetto, my father.

Anyone who was down on his luck and needed a place to stay—if they'd just come to America, just lost their job, or been thrown out of their house by an angry spouse—knew that my father would make room for them in our place. I was always coming out of the bedroom I shared with my brother to see a relative or a stranger sleeping on a sofa, staying for a few days or weeks. My father never asked for favors in return. He figured that the people who came into our home made our lives richer, too.

One night, we heard a commotion in our family grocery store downstairs. Some man had gotten drunk and tried to break in but was too drunk to know quite how to do it. My father crept downstairs and found that the man had slipped and knocked himself out cold, tripping over some egg crates. Some master thief.

We called the police. They told my father that if he pressed charges, they'd have to put the failed robber in jail. My father sighed and walked over to the man.

"Do you have a job?" he asked.

The man shook his head no, too embarrassed to speak.

Then my father told him, "Well, you have one now. You can work for me if you want to." And he did.

My father didn't do it out of pity. He truly felt that we had been blessed in America and were obliged to share our blessings with those who were less fortunate.

After all these years I can still trace how my father's love of the arts, music, and justice made their way into me. I remember how once he took me by the hand and we walked along the East River. We looked up into the sky and saw a dazzling display of soft colors, bright lights, and perfect, delicate, wavy shapes against the deep blackness. My father explained that it was something called the aurora borealis, and it was the greatest show on Earth. But you could see it only at certain times—it depended on the rotation of the planets and the weather—and it was therefore a great event to see it. It was the universe, lifting the flap a little to let us see how it worked, and the aurora reminded us that we are connected to the stars.

I'd have a dream in my childhood, too: that I was walking through tall green mountains, my hand in my father's, when we beheld a valley that brimmed with bright colors, like the ones we had seen in the sky. I felt at peace and at one with a huge world.

I like to think that dream motivated me to become a painter. I know it made me see that I shared a special view of the world with my father.

He'd read to us at night from some of the great classics of the time. The one I remember best is Somerset Maugham's 1915 novel *Of Human Bondage*, about a child born with a clubfoot who must make his way in life over ignorance and bigotry. Looking back on it now, I think that the books and arts my father loved best carried the theme of social justice and humanism in which he truly believed and by which he tried to live his life.

My father read about and admired Mahatma Gandhi and the movement for independence and peace he led against the British Empire, as well as Paul Robeson, an eloquent artist and advocate for justice in the United States. Our neighborhood in Queens was home to Italian families like ours but also to Irish, Italian, Jewish, and African American families. My father taught us that people were people, and all deserved respect.

My father loved show business. He'd take my brother, John, and me to movies, where we first saw (and learned to sing along with) Al Jolson. We'd finish dinner and settle in by the radio for hours to listen to Jolson and the great Eddie Cantor. My father had taste. He applauded anyone's effort to entertain. But he taught us to appreciate the professionalism of a Jolson or a Cantor, performers who kept going year after year, learning more as they went along.

But year after year, my father's health grew worse and worse. It hurts me to recount his pains now. His damaged heart valves might be easily repaired these days, but in Astoria, Queens, in 1936, there was not much more doctors could do than look on and tell our family to hope for the best and be brave.

My father spent a lot of time in the hospital on Governors Island. His heart would swell and crowd against his lungs late at night, trapping fluids inside his chest, which would make him gasp and moan. It is frightening for a little boy to see the man he knows is the strongest in the world, the man put on this Earth to protect and look out for him, wheeze and cry out in pain.

I'd cry out myself, asking, "Oh, God, Ma, what's happening?" My mother would be with my father, trying to ease his pain, and tell me that he would be all right and I certainly would. But I'd fall back to sleep, shivering.

I remember one night when my father got up from his bed with sheer willpower and stepped toward the bathroom with dignity. I was in the hallway, eager to see him. He took one laborious step after another to come over to me and put his arms around me.

"I love you," he said softly. "I love you."

To this day, I remember the caress in his arms and in his voice. He told us all how he loved us all the time. But that night, he must have known it was important for us to hold his love close.

My father was often so sick that by the time I was nine and ten, he'd have to be rushed to the hospital in the middle of the night. But one night, the hacking and wheezing and weakness were worse than ever. My father was rushed to the hospital, but this time they said he'd had congestive heart failure and pneumonia. He slipped into a semiconscious state.

I'd go to the hospital to visit my father every day. The nurses would have drawn the shades so that he could sleep. I'd sit by my father in the feeble light of a darkened room and hold his hand, hoping and praying that my touch could give him some strength, as his arms had given peace and protection to me.

Amazingly, he regained consciousness after three days. He suddenly grew so alert and alive that the doctors told us he would be able to come home the next day. We went home in a state of elation. We put new sheets on his bed and prepared for his homecoming.

But when we arrived at the hospital the next morning, the

nurses took us over into a corner of the vast waiting room. A doctor came out to tell us that my father had died in the middle of the night. He'd suffered another bout of congestive heart failure, and nothing they could do could free his lungs of the backup of fluid or the pain. My father was gone at the age of forty-one—a sensitive soul, a beautiful man, a lover of life and his family, gone from our lives forever.

Except, of course, no father ever is. Death doesn't do away with the connection you feel or the influence a parent has on you. In fact, I think it makes you cherish and treasure who they were and what they tried to tell you even more. Their death can make you seek out the lessons they have to give you, because you know it's your legacy.

My father taught me to love art, respect all kinds of people, strive for justice, and greet life with a song. I think he also showed me, in the short time he was with us, how to grow into a man: work hard, keep your word, care about others, and be interested in the world.

Once I could see I might have some talent worth pursuing, I decided to become a singer so that my mother would never, ever, have to sew another dress, run a needle through her thumb, and lug bags of dresses in her arms on long train rides to support us. Looking back on my ninety years now, I think I also became a singer to try to care for my mother in the way my father wanted to himself.

Over the decades, I've often tried to imagine my father as the young Giovanni Benedetto, climbing a mountain in Calabria and singing out into the valley. A few years ago, on a visit to Calabria, I was inspired to pay him a kind of tribute with that thought in my mind. I stood on the side of a mountain that looked out over a gorgeous green valley and I began to sing,

"O sole mio . . ." I heard my voice bounce from hill to hill and spread through the valley, and heard the words come back from the hills into my ears. I thought of the young boy, weak with sickness but filled with courage, grace, and love, who sang those same words into those same hills, sailed across an ocean to America, and filled a family with his love. My father gave me his voice, and I've tried to use it well.

Puerto Rico

Acknowledgments

Scott Simon, whose magnificent writing, full of intelligence and eloquence, was essential to this project.

My son and manager Danny Bennett, and the entire RPM Productions team: Sylvia Weiner, Hadley Spanier, Dawn Olejar, Sandi Rogers, and Susan Kerner, for all their support and hard work.

HarperCollins for their continued and valued association over the years, and especially Lisa Sharkey and Amy Bendell.

Mel Berger, from WME, for all his help with this project.

My quartet and crew, who travel the world with me: Gray Sargent, Harold Jones, Marshall Wood, Tom Young, John Callahan, and Ron Farino.

My wonderful wife, Susan Benedetto, who makes every day beautiful for me.

Dick Golden for his invaluable friendship.

My dear friend Jimmy Breslin for his kind words.

And to all the colleagues, family, and friends who are depicted in this book and have enriched my life.

Endpaper Artwork

Front Endpaper (from top left to bottom right):

Fred Astaire

Young Satchmo

Frank Sinatra

Lady Gaga

Pearl Bailey

Golden Gate Bridge

Ella Fitzgerald

Duke Ellington

Abraham Lincoln

Back Endpaper (from top left to bottom right):

Cary Grant

Louis Prima

Endpaper Artwork

San Francisco Cable Car

Charlie Chaplin

Bill Evans

Louis Armstrong

George Burns

Susan Benedetto and Boo

Rosemary Clooney

John Benedetto

About the Author

The child of Italian immigrants, TONY BENNETT grew up in Astoria, Queens, during the Great Depression. After serving as an infantryman in World War II, he studied singing and signed with Columbia Records in 1950, releasing his first hit with the label in 1951. Over the course of his career, which has spanned more than sixty years, he has sold millions of albums that have achieved gold and platinum status both in the United States and worldwide, and has won nineteen Grammy Awards. On August 3, 2016, Tony turned ninety.

SCOTT SIMON is the *New York Times* bestselling author of *Unforgettable: A Son, a Mother, and the Lessons of a Lifetime.* He is one of America's most admired writers and broadcasters, having reported from all over the world and from many wars. He is now the award-winning host of *Weekend Edition Saturday.* With more than four million listeners, it is the most-listened-to news program on National Public Radio. Simon has won Peabody and Emmy awards for his reporting.